WHY YOU ARE NOT BEHIND

The Science of

First-Generation

Black Wealth

by

BRIAN B. TURNER

For permissions, inquiries, or bulk orders, please contact:

hi@heybbt.com
www.heybbt.com

First Edition.
ISBN: 979-8-9937162-6-8

Printed in the United States of America

Table of Contents

361

PREFACE

A Truth We Were Never Taught

I began writing this book because of a moment that caught me off guard. I was not searching for a deep revelation. I was not studying economics or thinking about the past. I was sitting at a bar in Miami, headphones on, working on my laptop, the way many Black first-generation builders live. Focused. Tired. Managing a life that never seems to take its foot off the gas.

A stranger started a conversation with me.
His story came with access. Education. Opportunity. Movement. Legacy. He spoke about buying a home in Miami Beach years ago that is now worth more than most people will earn in their lifetime. He described it with a calmness that felt almost impossible to imagine for someone who grew up in the world I grew up in.

It was the calm that stayed with me.
Not the money.
Not the status.
Not the home.

The calm.

Because for so many of us, money has never been calm.
Money has been pressure.
Money has been calculation.

Money has been urgency.
Money has been a quiet storm running underneath every decision we make.

In that moment, while this man talked freely about a life that had never been shaped by economic delay, something clicked for me.

The issue was not that he was ahead.
The issue was that many of us began the race much later.

I realized something that took me decades to understand.
Something no one ever explained clearly.
Something that would have changed the way I saw myself, my progress, and my worth.

I was not behind.
I was first.

And so are many of us.

We are the first generation in our families with real access to the tools that build wealth.
Not imaginary access.
Not symbolic access.
Actual access.
Education. Homeownership possibilities. Business opportunities. Digital pathways. Careers that did not exist for our parents or grandparents.

We inherited the responsibility to move forward without inheriting the head start that many others received through property, protection, capital, law, geography, and time.

No one prepared us for the psychological weight of being the first.
No one told us how much pressure is created when you try to catch up to people who inherited the ability to compound while your family inherited survival.
No one explained how history shapes our timeline.
No one broke down why being first often feels like being late.

Instead, we were taught to judge ourselves.
We were given stereotypes instead of context.
We were handed opinions instead of the truth.
We were blamed for starting behind without any acknowledgment of how the starting line was built.

That is why this book exists.

Not to complain.
Not to cast blame.
Not to create excuses.
Not to recycle trauma.

This book exists to provide clarity.
Clarity about history.
Clarity about psychology.
Clarity about the delay.
Clarity about opportunity.
Clarity about the truth of Black first-generation wealth builders in America.

For the first time in our history, we have tools that can collapse timelines.
We have information at our fingertips.
We have visibility into industries that were previously hidden.
We have digital platforms that allow us to create our own opportunities.
We have access that previous generations would have considered impossible.

This book is here to help us understand the journey behind us and the possibilities ahead of us.

Because once you understand the real timeline, the shame dissolves.
Once you understand the delay, the pressure shifts.
Once you understand the weight you inherited, you stop seeing yourself as someone who is late.
You start seeing yourself as someone who is beginning.

That is the purpose of this book.

To correct the narrative.
To replace confusion with truth.
To replace comparison with clarity.
To replace guilt with understanding.
To replace the feeling of being behind with the reality of being early.

This book is for every Black person who has ever felt like they should be farther in life and could not understand why the journey felt so heavy.

You are not behind.
You were never behind.
You are the beginning.

And beginnings take time.

— Brian B. Turner

INTRODUCTION

The Real Story of Our Starting Line

Black people in America have spent generations trying to measure progress without understanding the truth about the race we entered. We have been told we are behind, yet no one ever explained how the track was built or when we were finally allowed on it. We learned to judge ourselves without understanding the timeline that shaped our lives.

This book begins by correcting that misunderstanding.

The idea that Black people should be farther than we are is not based on science. It is not based on history. It is not based on economics. It is based on a comparison that ignores the reality of our starting point.

To understand why you feel behind, you first have to understand the truth about the beginning.

For most Black families in America, wealth building is not a continuation of previous generations. It is not a handoff. It is not a tradition. It is not a steady climb. It is a beginning. A fresh start. A first attempt. A first generation trying to build what previous generations were denied.

That is not a flaw.
That is a fact.
And the facts matter.

When economists study wealth patterns, they describe wealth as something that grows through time. Wealth compounds when assets are passed down, when property values rise, when networks open doors, and when money earns money. Wealth grows when time does the work. Families that own homes, land, businesses, investments, and capital pass advantages forward. Their children do not begin from zero. They begin from a foundation.

Black Americans were shut out of that foundation for more than two centuries.
Not by chance.
By design.

Slavery created zero capital.
Jim Crow blocked access to opportunity.
Redlining prevented homeownership and generational equity.
Mass incarceration removed earning power and stability from entire communities.

This is not a political statement. This is historical data. Every time Black wealth began to grow, a system intervened. As a result, most Black families did not start wealth building when other families did. Our compounding began late. Our access began late. Our stability began late.

So when you look at your life and think you should be farther along, you are comparing yourself to families whose timelines started long before yours. You are comparing your first chapter to someone else's fourth or fifth. You are comparing progress to inheritance.

Once you understand the timeline, everything changes.

You stop asking what is wrong with you.
You stop carrying guilt for not having what others inherited.
You stop assuming your pace reflects your potential.
You stop believing you are behind.
You realize you are the beginning.

This is not only about economics. This is about identity, history, and the weight we inherited.

My position in this conversation is simple.
I have seen this story from the inside, and I have studied it from the outside, and that perspective is what I am offering you here.

This book exists to explain the beginning clearly.

Not with excuses.
Not with anger.
Not with blame.
Not with slogans.
Not with emotional arguments.

With clarity.
With truth.
With structure.
With history.
With science.
With the psychology of first-generation wealth building.
With the opportunities that exist today.
With a realistic blueprint for what comes next.

Being first-generation means you are building a foundation that will support the generations that follow you. It means you are carrying responsibilities that your parents and grandparents could not carry. It means you are navigating paths they were never allowed to enter. It means your mistakes feel heavier and your progress feels slower because you are building a life without a template.

It also means something powerful.
You are the first one to have access to information that can accelerate everything. You are the first with technology. You are the first with a global marketplace. You are the first with digital tools that can collapse timelines. You are the first generation with the ability to rewrite what wealth looks like in our community.

This book is here to show you why the journey feels the way it feels, and why the feeling does not match the truth. It will connect the historical delay, the psychological weight, the economic patterns, the cultural narratives, and the modern opportunities into one clear picture.

By the end, you will understand why your timeline looks different. You will understand why your progress feels invisible. You will understand why your journey has felt heavier. You will understand why none of that means you are behind.

You will understand that you are early.

And once you see the truth, you can finally build without shame, without confusion, and without comparison.

Welcome to the real story of your starting line. Welcome to the beginning.

Chapter 1: Born Into the Delay

Understanding the First-Generation Black Wealth Timeline

Every generation begins somewhere.
Some begin on solid ground.
Some begin with a structure already in place.
Some begin with wealth, working quietly in the background.
Some begin with land, guidance, and networks that open doors without effort.
Some begin with the confidence that comes from knowing they will not fall too far.

Most Black Americans began somewhere else entirely.
We began in a delay built long before we were born.

A delay that shaped our homes.
A delay that shaped our schools.
A delay that shaped our opportunities.
A delay that shaped our psychology.
A delay that shaped the expectations placed on us.
A delay we were told to ignore, even as we carried its weight.

To understand why you feel behind, you must understand the delay that came before you.
A delay is not an excuse.
A delay is a measurement.

A delay is a timeline.
A delay is a truth that explains the pressure you have spent your entire life trying to interpret.

You cannot understand your progress without understanding where your race began.

Most families in America who hold wealth today have been compounding it for several generations. Wealth is not simply money. Wealth is time. Wealth is accumulation. Wealth is protection. Wealth is what happens when assets sit still long enough to grow.

Economists call this "intergenerational compounding."
Time does the heavy lifting.
Equity increases while no one is looking.
Land appreciates while people sleep.
Stocks grow while families age.
Businesses expand because they are not being built in panic.
Networks guide children toward opportunity without calling it a strategy.
These forces work quietly, invisibly, and steadily.

They create security.
They create upward mobility.
They create a baseline.

Most Black families never had that baseline.
Not because we lacked ambition or discipline or intelligence.

But because our timeline was interrupted at every stage where compounding was supposed to begin.

Slavery prevented capital accumulation.
Jim Crow prevented access to opportunity.
Redlining prevented homeownership and inheritance.
Mass incarceration destabilized families and stripped economic power from entire communities.

These are not emotional claims.
These are documented economic events.

Slavery removed 246 years of labor, property ownership, literacy, and legal personhood from our family lines.
Jim Crow removed 90 years of political and economic access.
Redlining wiped out 40 years of home equity growth during the very decades when white middle-class wealth exploded.
Mass incarceration removed millions of Black men and women from the workforce, the community, and the home during the peak earning years of their lives.

These four events created more than a gap.
They created a **reset** every time our community began to rise.
They created a **delay** that no amount of personal hard work could outpace in a single lifetime.

When you inherit a delay, your life feels different.
Not weaker. Different.
Not less ambitious. Different.
Not less capable. Different.

You are not building on a foundation.
You are building a foundation.

Most Americans do not start from zero.
Most Black Americans did.

When you are building from zero, progress feels slow because you are doing the work of several generations at once.
You are stabilizing your present while building your future.
You are managing survival and strategy at the same time.
You are carrying the weight of being first without anyone telling you that is what you are doing.

This creates a psychological reality that is rarely discussed.

First-generation wealth builders experience more self-doubt.
First-generation wealth builders experience more pressure to succeed quickly.
First-generation wealth builders experience more fear of failure.
First-generation wealth builders experience more guilt when they rest.
First-generation wealth builders experience more

urgency around every decision.
First-generation wealth builders experience more emotional triggers around money.
First-generation wealth builders feel the consequences of mistakes more intensely.

These patterns are not flaws.
They are symptoms of the delay.

When people say, "Black people should be farther," they are ignoring every structural force that determines how wealth forms. They are ignoring the centuries when our families were denied the right to accumulate. They are ignoring the decades when our neighborhoods were devalued. They are ignoring the policies that created the middle class for others and closed the doors for us. They are ignoring the fact that compounding cannot begin when the starting point is survival.

This is not hopeless.
It is context.
And context creates clarity.

Understanding the delay does not weaken your ambition.
It sharpens it.
It gives you a realistic view of the race you are running.
It removes shame from your timeline.
It explains why your progress feels heavy.
It removes the belief that something is wrong with you.

It reveals that something was wrong with the starting line.

Every generation inherits something.
You inherited the responsibility to begin.

Being first-generation means you are the first to access information that your family was denied.
You are the first to navigate industries that were once hidden.
You are the first to move through systems that were once closed.
You are the first to build without the scaffolding that supports others.
You are the first to create a future your ancestors could only imagine.

This responsibility is weighty, and it should be acknowledged.
Not to create limits, but to release guilt.
Not to weaken you, but to strengthen your self-understanding.
Not to soften your ambition, but to make it more precise.

You are not falling behind.
You are catching up to yourself.
You are building what should have been handed to you.
You are starting a race that began before you could walk.
You are doing the work of generations in real time.
You are the opening chapter of your family's wealth

story.
You are the first heartbeat in a lineage that is learning to rise.

Once you see the delay clearly, you begin to see yourself clearly.
You stop measuring your life against timelines that don't belong to you.
You stop punishing yourself for the years you spent surviving.
You stop telling yourself that you should be further.
You begin to honor the truth.
You are the foundation.
You are the origin.
You are the one who begins the compounding that will benefit your children and grandchildren.

You were born into a delay.
But you were also born into the first era in which that delay could be overcome.

Technology.
Information.
Digital access.
Global markets.
Education.
Mobility.
Opportunity.

These tools make you the first Black generation to have the ability to end the delay and begin the compounding.

That is why this book exists.
To show you that the weight you carry has a cause.
To show you that the pressure you feel has a source.
To show you that the timeline you have been
judging yourself against was never yours.
To show you that you are not behind.
You are the beginning.

And the beginning is powerful.

Chapter 2: The Four Breaks

How History Interrupted the Black Wealth Timeline

Wealth does not begin with money.
Wealth begins with stability.
Wealth begins with safety.
Wealth begins with the ability to own, to keep, and to pass something forward.

For most Black families in America, that ability was interrupted long before any of us were born. Not by natural events. Not by poor decisions. Not by cultural habits. But by four structural breaks that cut the timeline of wealth every time it tried to form.

These breaks are not stories from another era.
These breaks shaped the world you were born into.
These breaks created the delay you inherited.

They created the four interruptions that define the Black wealth timeline:

1. Slavery

2. Jim Crow

3. Redlining

4. Mass incarceration

If you remove emotion, remove politics, and look at these events as economists do, you see a single truth:

Black Americans were prevented from entering the compounding stage of wealth for more than three centuries.

This chapter explains how.

---

1. Slavery: The Theft of Time, Labor, and Capital

Slavery was not only a system of forced labor.
It was a system designed to prevent the creation of wealth.

Economically, three variables build wealth:

- labor

- ownership

- time

Slavery removed all three.

Black people could not own land.
Black people could not earn wages.
Black people could not keep assets.

Black people could not legally hold value.
Black people could not pass anything forward.

Every hour of labor held zero economic return.
Every year of life created zero compounding.
Every generation ended exactly where it started.

From a wealth perspective, slavery was not simply oppression.
It was a complete freeze.
A forced reset that lasted 246 years.

If wealth is measured across time, and time was stolen, there was nothing to inherit.

This is the beginning of the delay.

---

2. Jim Crow: The Blocked Path

Freedom without access is not freedom.
It is a new form of limitation.

Jim Crow replaced physical chains with institutional ones.
It controlled movement.
It controlled education.
It controlled housing.
It controlled employment.
It controlled safety.
It controlled capital.

Economically, this meant:

- low wages

- unstable employment

- limited schooling

- segregated neighborhoods

- restricted mobility

- no legal protection

- no access to growth industries

Jim Crow robbed Black families of the first 90 years after slavery, when America experienced massive economic expansion.

While white families accumulated property, built businesses, and entered new professions, Black families were still fighting for permission to participate.

The delay widened again.

---

3. Redlining: The Destroyed Middle Class

Between the 1930s and 1970s, homeownership became the engine of American middle-class

wealth.
Home values increased steadily.
Neighborhoods appreciated.
Equity grew quietly in the background.

The majority of white families entered this period early.
Black families were pushed out of it entirely.

Through federal housing policies, banks marked Black neighborhoods as "hazardous," which meant:

- no loans

- no mortgages

- no credit

- no investment

- no rising property values

This meant:
White families built equity.
Black families built rent receipts.

White families passed homes to their children.
Black families passed nothing forward, even when they worked just as hard.

Economists estimate redlining alone prevented up to **$200 billion** in Black generational wealth from being created.

The delay deepened again.

---

4. Mass Incarceration: The Interrupted Household

Beginning in the 1980s, Black communities
experienced a different loss.
This time, it was not exclusion.
It was extraction.

Mass incarceration removed Black men and women
from the economy during their prime working
years.
It destroyed:

- income

- household stability

- savings

- parental presence

- educational outcomes for children

- community networks

- future earning potential

A generation that could have begun compounding was instead criminalized.

This was not random.
It was policy-driven.
And the economic impact is measurable.

Removing millions of people from the workforce for decades did not only punish individuals.
It destabilized the entire wealth-building structure of Black America.

And the delay stretched again.

What These Four Breaks Created

When combined, these four events did something unique:

They eliminated the first, second, third, and fourth chances for Black wealth to begin.

Other families had:

- time

- land

- wages

- safe communities

- functioning schools

- access to capital

- business opportunities

- low-interest mortgages

- legal protection

- uninterrupted family structures

Black families did not.

By the time the doors to America's wealth engine finally opened, the starting line had already been set.

The gap was not a failure.
The gap was a timeline.

This is why comparing Black progress to other groups has always been inaccurate.
You cannot compare generations that inherited compounding to generations that inherited resets.

The delay is not a metaphor.
It is math.
It is sociology.
It is public policy.
It is generational psychology.
It is American design.

And understanding it changes everything.

Why This History Matters Today

You are not reading this book to learn about the past.
You are reading it to understand your present.

When you feel pressure around money, you are not imagining it.
When you feel late, you are not imagining it.
When you feel behind in homeownership, business, investing, or career movement, you are not imagining it.

You are living inside a timeline shaped by interruption.

Most Black people today are the first generation with:

- full legal access

- technology

- mobility

- visibility

- global markets

- financial education

- entrepreneurial possibility

We are the first generation to have the ability to begin compounding.

That does not mean the past is your prison.
It means the past explains your starting point.

This history is not here to weigh you down.
It is here to free you from false conclusions about yourself.

You were not behind.
You were not slow.
You were not late.
You were not unprepared.
You were not less capable.
You were born into a delay.
That delay had a cause.
And now it has an end.

The purpose of this book is not to relive those four breaks.
The purpose is to show you what it means to live beyond them.

You are the first generation standing on the edge of a new beginning.
And beginnings are powerful.

Chapter 3: The Psychology of Being First

Why the Journey Feels Heavier Than the Truth

There is a moment every first-generation Black wealth builder experiences.
It is not a moment you can circle on a calendar.
It is not a moment anyone prepares you for.
It is not something discussed openly.

It is the moment when you realize you are working toward something your family has never seen.
You are trying to build a life without a reference point.
You are trying to make progress without a model.
You are trying to break cycles while carrying their weight.

This chapter explains the quiet truth:
Being the first is not only a financial responsibility.
It is a psychological one.

You are not only building wealth.
You are building identity.
You are building stability.
You are building belief.
You are building vision.
You are building possibilities for the generations that follow you.

This creates a unique emotional landscape that very few people understand.

1. The Pressure of Being the First to Figure It Out

Most people grow up seeing wealth behaviors modeled:

- how to save

- how to invest

- how to use credit responsibly

- how to buy a home

- how to build networks

- how to navigate high-income environments

- how to recover after financial mistakes

First-generation Black builders do not have that.
You are learning and being judged in real time.
You are expected to perform without guidance.
You are expected to rise without instruction.
You are expected to succeed without seeing what success looks like.

This creates a psychological pattern that therapists identify as **survival-driven decision-making**.

You make financial choices with urgency because you have never experienced financial safety.
You internalize mistakes more deeply because no one taught you how to recover from them.
You attach your self-worth to your income because income has always equaled survival.

This pressure is not personal.
It is inherited.

---

2. The Fear of Falling Backward

When you are the first to rise, you live with a quiet fear that everything you are building can collapse.
This fear does not come from paranoia.
It comes from history.

You come from generations who lived one crisis away from disaster.
Generations who had no cushion.
Generations who had no safety net.
Generations who had no backup plan.
Generations who learned to adapt to loss because they were never allowed to build protection.

This fear lives in your nervous system even when your bank account improves.
It whispers that success is temporary.
It whispers that one mistake can undo everything.
It whispers that stability is fragile.

Psychologists call this **intergenerational scarcity wiring**.
It makes you more conservative in some moments and more impulsive in others.
It makes rest feel dangerous.
It makes ambition feel risky.
It makes progress feel reversible.

This fear is not a flaw.
It is an imprint.

---

3. The Hidden Grief of Being First

Being the first generation to rise comes with a form of grief many do not recognize.
You grieve the guidance you never received.
You grieve the stability you did not grow up with.
You grieve the opportunities you had to discover on your own.
You grieve the childhood you would have had if your parents had what you are trying to build now.
You grieve the years lost to survival.
You grieve the innocence lost to reality.

This grief does not stop you.
It shapes you.

It turns you into someone who feels responsible for carrying your family forward.
It makes you the emotional, financial, and

psychological anchor for people who never received the support they needed.

This burden is real.
And it is heavy.

---

4. The Weight of Dual Identity

First-generation Black wealth builders live in two worlds.

In one world, you are trying to elevate your life.
In the other, you are connected to people who are still surviving.

You feel responsible for both worlds.
You feel guilty for wanting more.
You feel guilty for achieving more.
You feel torn between advancing yourself and supporting your family.
You feel pressure to succeed for people who never had the chance.

Sociologists call this **dual-identity strain**.
It creates emotional exhaustion because you are trying to hold two realities at once.

You cannot separate them.
You carry both.

---

5. The Loneliness of Climbing Without Peers

When you are first-generation, you often rise alone.
Your friends may not be climbing at the same pace.
Your family may not understand your goals.
Your coworkers may not share your background.
Your mentors may not exist yet.
Your community may pull you down or lift you up randomly.

Loneliness becomes part of your journey.
Not because something is wrong with you.
But because you are moving into spaces your lineage has never entered.

There is no map for this.
There is no familiar face.
There is no guided path.
You are walking into the unknown while people around you assume you should already know what you are doing.

This is the psychological cost of being the first.

---

6. The Silence Around Your Stress

Black first-generation builders are rarely allowed to verbalize their stress.
You do not want to seem ungrateful.

You do not want to seem weak.
You do not want to seem incapable.
You do not want to reinforce stereotypes.
You do not want to disappoint people who believe in you.

So you carry your stress quietly.
You succeed loudly and struggle privately.
You celebrate small wins while hiding overwhelming pressure.
You keep moving because you believe stopping would dishonor the sacrifices of those who came before you.

This silence is not a choice.
It is a survival pattern.

---

7. The Burden of Breaking Cycles

Cycle breaking is not motivational.
It is mechanical.
It is emotional.
It is exhausting.

You are not only trying to advance yourself.
You are trying to repair what was damaged, replace what was missing, and build what never existed.

Cycle breaking requires:

- emotional healing

- financial literacy

- responsibility without guidance

- maturity without modeling

- discipline without support

- vision without precedent

This is why the journey feels overwhelming.
You are doing the work of multiple generations in one lifetime.
Economists call this **compressed generational uplift**.

It is heavy.
And it is heroic.

---

8. The Truth That Changes Everything

The feelings you carry are not symptoms of weakness.
They are symptoms of being first.

You feel pressure because you are building without a template.
You feel fear because your lineage taught you what

instability feels like.

You feel grief because you are healing what was never healed.

You feel lonely because you are rising faster than your reference points.

You feel stress because you inherited the responsibility to begin.

This chapter exists to tell you something you have never been told:

Your psychology makes sense.
Your struggle makes sense.
Your emotions make sense.
Your pace makes sense.
You make sense.

You are not behind.
You are carrying a generation forward.
You are the first link in a new chain.
You are the beginning of stability.
You are the foundation of your family's future.
You are the one who ends the delay.

Chapter 3 tells you why the journey feels heavy.
Chapter 4 will tell you how to move through it with clarity.

You are not late.
You are early.
And being early often feels like being alone.

Until you understand the truth.

Chapter 4: The Myth of the Bootstrap

Why Hard Work Alone Does Not Build Wealth in America

Every first-generation Black wealth builder grows up hearing the same message:

Work hard.
Do the right things.
Make good choices.
Stay out of trouble.
Get an education.
Save your money.
Life will reward you.

It sounds noble.
It sounds empowering.
It sounds fair.

But for millions of Black Americans, it has never been true.

Not because we lack discipline.
Not because we lack desire.
Not because we lack intelligence.
Not because we lack work ethic.
Not because we lack ambition.

It is not true because wealth in America has never been built on hard work alone.

Wealth has always been built on **hard work plus structure**.

Structure is what multiplies effort.
Structure is what protects progress.
Structure is what turns income into stability.
Structure is what amplifies small decisions over time.
Structure is what converts possibility into legacy.

This chapter exposes one of the most damaging myths ever sold to Black America:
the belief that personal effort can overcome structural timelines.

It cannot.
Not alone.

Not historically.
Not mathematically.
Not psychologically.
Not generationally.

This is the truth almost no one will say out loud.

**1. Hard Work Produces Wages.

Structure Produces Wealth.**

Every hour you work produces income.
But income does not produce wealth unless there are tools in place to grow it.

These tools include:

- property

- credit

- inherited stability

- early financial education

- healthy networks

- business access

- low-interest capital

- community support

- safety

- time

Most Black families were denied these tools for centuries.
So even when we worked harder than any group in American history, we still did not produce generational wealth.

Hard work without structure is survival.
Hard work with structure is legacy.

This is the secret America never teaches.

2. Other Groups Did Not Bootstrap Their Way to Wealth

White Americans did not build wealth by working harder.
They built wealth through:

- free land grants

- government-subsidized loans

- low-interest mortgages

- protected neighborhoods

- exclusive unions

- college admissions pipelines

- corporate hiring networks

- business-friendly policies

- consistent legal protection

- inherited assets

- compounding over time

This is not an attack.
It is a timeline.

America gave white families the structure they needed to build wealth.
America gave Black families advice.

"Work hard and stop complaining."

But if hard work built wealth,
slavery would have made Black people the richest group in the country.

It did not.

Because wealth is not built by labor alone.
It is built on access, stability, compounding, and time.

---

3. The Psychological Impact of the Bootstrap Lie

Telling Black people that hard work alone creates wealth does something damaging:

It turns structural delay into personal blame.

You begin to think:
"I should be farther."
"I must be doing something wrong."
"I did everything they told me to do. Why is my life

still this hard?"
"I should not be stressed."
"I should be more successful by now."

You internalize struggle as a personal failure rather than a structural inheritance.

This creates:

- shame

- anxiety

- impostor syndrome

- financial guilt

- quiet depression

- burnout

- self-blame

- emotional exhaustion

The lie becomes a weapon you use against yourself. It becomes a voice inside you saying:

"You are behind because you are not enough."

This book exists to end that lie.

4. The Blueprint You Were Never Given

White America did not keep wealth a secret. They simply did not teach Black families the blueprint.

The real wealth formula is simple:

1. **Start early**

2. **Own assets that appreciate**

3. **Protect those assets with stable environments**

4. **Use time to multiply value**

5. **Pass it down so the next generation starts ahead**

That is generational wealth.

This formula was never handed to us because none of the steps were accessible to us until recently. You cannot start early if your grandparents had nothing to start with. You cannot own appreciating assets if you were locked out of them. You cannot protect assets if your communities were destabilized. You cannot use time if every generation is forced to start over.

Bootstrapping works when the boots came with laces.
Ours did not.

We were told to pull ourselves up with instructions we were never given.

---

5. The Cultural Cost of Believing It Is All on You

Believing in the bootstrap myth creates cultural strain.

It leads to:

- overwork

- burnout

- perfectionism

- silence

- self-criticism

- fear of asking for help

- isolation

- unrealistic expectations

- pressure to "be the one"

- financial anxiety

It turns every Black success story into a miracle instead of a plan.
It turns every failure into a shameful secret instead of a structural reality.
It puts unrealistic pressure on the first few people to make it out.

It convinces you that rest is laziness.
It convinces you that struggle is your fault.
It convinces you that success must be earned the hardest way possible.

That is not freedom.
That is psychological bondage.

---

6. The Truth: It Is Not All on You

You cannot overcome 300 years of structural delay with personal effort alone.
You cannot compress five generations of stability into one lifetime without tools.
You cannot build wealth without structure.
You cannot protect progress without support.
You cannot build legacy on grit alone.

This does not make you weak.
It makes you human.

The truth is simple:

You are not behind.
You were never behind.
You were building without the very tools that other families were handed at birth.

Now that the tools are accessible, the narrative must change.

This chapter is not here to discourage you.
It is here to free you from the belief that your struggle is your fault.

You are not failing.
You are pioneering.
You are not slow.
You are starting from a place others never had to experience.
You are not lacking.
You are navigating a roadmap no one gave your family.

Hard work matters.
But structure determines destiny.

You are entering the first generation where structure finally exists.

And that changes everything.

Chapter 5: The Survival Tax

How Poverty, Stress, and Chaos Affect Wealth Decisions

There is a cost we never talk about.
A cost that never appears on a receipt, a bank statement, or a budget.
A cost that takes more from Black first-generation wealth builders than any bill or expense.

That cost is the **Survival Tax**.

It is the invisible tax imposed by stress, scarcity, chaos, instability, and the psychological burden of trying to build wealth while under pressure.

Other families pass down assets.
We pass down urgency.

Other families inherit safety.
We inherit survival.

And survival has a price.

This chapter explains that price, not as a metaphor or poetry, but as neuroscience, psychology, and behavioral economics. The decisions you made in a state of survival were not character flaws. They were predictable outcomes of cognitive strain.

Understanding this truth frees you from shame.
It reveals why so many of your financial choices
made perfect sense in the environment you were in.

---

1. Scarcity Shrinks the Mind

Economists Sendhil Mullainathan and Eldar Shafir
introduced the concept of **Scarcity Theory**.
Their research shows something profound:

When you grow up in or live inside poverty, your
brain becomes focused on immediate needs.
Not because you are irresponsible.
Because your mind is trying to protect you.

Scarcity:

- narrows attention

- reduces cognitive bandwidth

- increases impulsive decisions

- decreases long-term planning

- raises stress hormones

- reduces executive function

This is measurable.
Brain scans show that chronic stress literally changes how the mind operates.

When you do not feel safe, long-term thinking becomes a luxury.
Your brain focuses on right now.

This is why so many Black first-generation builders:

- take safe jobs instead of strategic ones

- delay investing

- stay in environments that feel familiar

- avoid risk

- jump at quick income

- struggle with consistency

- feel overwhelmed by planning

- make decisions that seem irrational later

Your mind was not broken.
Your conditions were.

2. Chaos Taxes Your Future

Many Black families grow up in environments filled with unpredictability:

- unstable homes

- unpredictable income

- inconsistent support

- family crises

- violence

- school instability

- unsafe neighborhoods

- constant adaptation

Chaos forces the brain to spend energy on immediate survival.

This creates what psychologists call **cognitive load**, taxing future thinking.

Chaos teaches you:

- to react, not plan

- to adapt, not prepare

- to respond, not strategize

- to survive, not invest

- to fix problems, not prevent them

When your childhood taught you to anticipate danger, your adulthood taught you to anticipate bills, setbacks, and emergencies.

This keeps your decision-making in "defensive mode," even when your income rises.

You are not behind.
You are unlearning survival.

---

3. Stress Changes Your Financial Behavior

Long-term stress does not only affect your emotions, it affects your decisions.

Stress:

- lowers patience

- increases impulsive spending

- increases fear around investing

- makes money feel heavier

- reduces future orientation

- increases mistakes

- weakens discipline

- heightens risk aversion

These are **human responses**, not cultural flaws.

When you live under constant pressure, your brain prioritizes relief over growth.

That is why many first-generation Black builders say: "I know better, so why don't I do better?"
Because knowing and doing require different mental states.

Stress pushes you toward survival behaviors.
Stability pushes you toward wealth behaviors.

You simply have not had enough stability yet.

---

4. Trauma Rewrites Your Relationship with Money

Trauma is not only emotional.
It becomes behavioral.

Growing up in scarcity teaches you:

- money disappears

- money is unpredictable

- money causes conflict

- money is stressful

- money is survival

So when you finally earn money, you may:

- spend it quickly

- save excessively

- fear losing it

- feel unworthy of it

- avoid looking at finances

- attach identity to income

- feel pressure to help family

- feel guilty for wanting luxury

- overcompensate in generosity

These are not personal flaws.
They are survival imprints.

You are not fighting laziness.
You are fighting history in your nervous system.

---

5. The First-Gen Black Male Burden

The research shows something specific and intense:
When Black men rise economically, their psychological stress increases more than that of any other group.

Why?
Because they carry:

- the weight of being "the one"

- the fear of falling back

- the responsibility to help others

- the expectation to stay strong

- the pressure to succeed

- the silence about pain

- the trauma of instability

- the distrust formed by past environments

This combination creates a constant tension between ambition and fear.

Black men are often taught to grind harder, not heal deeper.
To muscle through, not understand the pressure.
To perform strength, not process stress.

This burden affects financial decisions.
It explains overwork, burnout, impatience, and moments of self-sabotage.

The struggle is not weakness.
It is the Survival Tax, multiplied.

---

6. Why You Are Not Behind…You Were Surviving

Every behavior you judge yourself for has a psychological explanation:

- The job you stayed in too long

- The investments you delayed

- The money you overspent

- The opportunities you avoided

- The risks you did not take

- The fear that slowed you down

You were not behind.
You were surviving.

You were using the mental model that kept your family alive.
You were using strategies designed for danger, not for stability.
You were functioning inside a mind shaped by scarcity, not abundance.

That was not your fault.
That was your environment.

Now that you have awareness, you can build differently.

---

7. The Shift Begins with Clarity

The moment you understand the Survival Tax, three things happen:

1. Your shame lifts.

2. Your self-judgment resets.

3. Your identity shifts from "behind" to "beginning."

You stop believing you are flawed.
You start understanding that you were conditioned.
You stop blaming yourself.
You start studying yourself.
You stop repeating patterns without knowing why.
You start designing new ones intentionally.

Clarity is liberation.
Awareness is transformation.

Survival taught you how to endure.
Now, stability will teach you how to rise.

Chapter 6: The Miseducation Machine

What Black America Was Never Taught About Wealth (And Why)

When we talk about why Black wealth lags behind, people often point to a lack of money.
But money was not the only thing taken.
Information was taken.
Direction was taken.
Blueprints were taken.
Confidence was taken.
Identity was taken.
Belief was taken.

Whole generations were raised inside systems designed to keep them working, not building.
Obedient, not empowered.
Productive, not prosperous.

Before Black Americans were denied wealth, we were denied the knowledge that creates wealth.

Not by accident.
By design.

This chapter explains the machine that shaped how you think about money, work, ownership, identity, freedom, and possibility.

It explains why you were not taught the very things that other families quietly passed down for generations.

It explains why even now, as a first-generation wealth builder, you sometimes feel like you are making it up as you go.

Because you are.

And it is not your fault.

---

1. School Was Never Designed to Teach You Wealth

Public education did not fail Black students.
It succeeded at its original purpose.

The American school system was never built to produce owners, investors, founders, creators, visionaries, strategists, or wealth builders.

It was built to produce:
workers, factory labor, predictable employees, people who follow rules, and people who do not question structure.

The system was designed during the Industrial Revolution for a world of bells, bosses, repetition, compliance, and uniformity.

Black children were placed into a system that was already outdated for building wealth.

We were taught to memorize, obey, complete assignments, and fit into existing structures.

But never how to build new structures.
Never how to create value.
Never how to grow assets.
Never how to use money as a tool.

You cannot build a wealthy future with a mindset built for a factory.

---

2. The Curriculum Left Out the Blueprint

Other communities teach wealth at home:

- how interest works

- how credit works

- how loans work

- how inheritance works

- how corporations work

- how taxes work

- how investing works

- how property works

- how networks work

Black families could not teach what they were denied.
So we grew up learning survival instead of strategy.

The Miseducation Machine filled the gap with distractions:

- memorize state capitals

- memorize dates

- memorize formulas

But nothing that explains:

- how wealth forms

- how wealth is protected

- how wealth is grown

- how wealth is passed down

- how wealth is multiplied

Children are shaped by what they are taught.
Black children were shaped by what they were not taught.

That was not an accident.

---

3. The Identity Miseducation

Carter G. Woodson wrote "The Mis-Education of the Negro" in 1933.
The brilliance of that work is still misunderstood.

Woodson was not only talking about schooling.
He was talking about identity.

The system taught Black children:

- who they were allowed to be

- how far they were allowed to go

- what roles they should play

- what jobs they should accept

- what dreams were acceptable

- what behavior was safe

It taught Black children to see themselves through a lens of limitation.
To operate inside boundaries.
To shrink their possibilities out of habit, not truth.

This identity miseducation becomes internalized.
It becomes a voice saying:
"Be careful.
Be realistic.
Stay safe.
Do not risk too much.
Do not dream too far."

The system not only failed to teach wealth, it taught fear.

---

4. The Economic Miseducation

Black Americans were intentionally excluded from:

- business education

- banking access

- entrepreneurship networks

- capital pipelines

- investment communities

So we learned to pursue:

- secure jobs

- stable checks

- predictable paths

Instead of:

- equity

- ownership

- scalability

- leverage

- financial independence

The Miseducation Machine produced generations of brilliant, hardworking, disciplined workers who were never taught how to convert effort into ownership.

Effort without ownership creates exhaustion. Ownership without effort creates legacy.

The machine ensured we remained on the wrong side of that equation.

---

5. The Cultural Miseducation

We were taught:

- pride without power

- resilience without resources

- ambition without access

- achievement without assets

- success without strategy

We were raised on messages like:
"You need to get a good job."
"Do not rock the boat."
"Be grateful you made it out."
"Stay humble."
"Be thankful."

None of those are wealth instructions.

Humility is good.
Gratitude is good.
Pride is good.

But none replace:

- ownership

- risk tolerance

- financial literacy

- creativity

- innovation

- real wealth psychology

Culture gave us values.
The machine removed the blueprint.

---

6. The Psychological Miseducation

If you teach a child long enough, that:

- opportunities are limited

- mistakes are dangerous

- failure is shameful

- money is unpredictable

- scarcity is normal

- ambition is risky

- wealth is suspicious

That child becomes an adult who:

- plays small

- doubts decisions

- fears investing

- chooses safety over ownership

- mistrusts wealth

- overworks

- undercharges

- hesitates when it matters most

This is not personal hesitation.
This is conditioned hesitation.

Your mind is not broken.
Your training was incomplete.

THE REAL REASON BLACK AMERICA WAS MISEDUCATED

The WHY They Never Wanted You To See

Black miseducation was not an accident.
It was not oversight.
It was not ignorance.
It was not a flaw in the system.

It was the system.

To understand why Black America was never taught wealth, you must see the truth clearly:

You cannot give wealth knowledge to a population with whom you do not intend to share wealth.

Black people were denied access to financial literacy because literacy fosters independence.
We were denied business education because ownership creates power.
We were denied economic truth because truth creates awareness.
We were denied wealth instruction because understanding the rules would have made us competitors.

We were taught to work, not build.
To follow, not own.
To succeed within the system, not question the system.
To perform excellence, not accumulate equity.

Why?

Because the American economy depended on Black labor, not Black liberation.

A population that understands:

- money

- systems

- power

- law

- capital

- inheritance

- compounding

cannot be controlled by fear, dependence, or limited opportunity.

The Miseducation Machine existed to maintain the hierarchy.
To preserve generational advantage.
To keep certain families rising while keeping others contained.

Black children were not miseducated because they lacked ability.

They were miseducated because they possessed possibility.

The system did not fear Black poverty.
It feared Black potential.

You were not kept uninformed because you were weak.
You were kept uninformed because you were powerful.

---

7. The Recovery Starts Now

The reason this chapter matters is simple:

You cannot build wealth with a blueprint you were never taught.
You cannot change direction with information you never received.
You cannot rise with a mindset designed to keep you contained.

Awareness is liberation.
Exposure is transformation.
Knowledge is power.
Self-understanding is currency.

This is the generation that breaks the Miseducation Machine.

Not by anger.
Not by blame.
By replacement.

We are replacing:
survival with strategy,
fear with literacy,
silence with clarity,
compliance with creativity,
limitation with ownership,
delay with direction.

This is the chapter where you meet the person you were supposed to be the entire time.

You were not behind.
You were never given the map.

Now you have it.

Chapter 7: The Comparison Trap

Why You Feel Behind (Even When You Are Not)

There is a quiet pain that almost every
first-generation Black wealth builder carries.
It does not come from failure.
It does not come from laziness.
It does not come from ignorance.
It comes from comparison.

Comparison is the invisible force that convinces you
your progress is inadequate.
It tells you the timeline you are living in is wrong.
It tells you someone your age should be further.
It tells you your wins are small and your pace is slow.
It tells you your life is behind the lives you see
around you.

You compare your beginning to someone else's
middle.
You compare your foundation to someone else's
inheritance.
You compare your survival to someone else's
structure.
You compare your lived reality to someone else's
highlight reel.

Comparison is not just mental.
It is psychological conditioning.

This chapter explains why comparison hits Black first-generation builders differently than it does other groups.

It is not insecurity.
It is history.
It is psychology.
It is identity.
And it is a trap.

---

1. Comparison Was Designed Into Your Experience

Comparison is not natural.
It is taught.

Black Americans were taught to compare themselves to people who benefited from 300 years of uninterrupted compounding.

We were taught to measure:

- progress without inheritance

- success without safety

- outcomes without protection

- pace without support

- achievement without guidance

We were placed in systems where our value was measured next to people with head starts.
We were graded on the same curve without the same starting line.
We were asked to perform in races that began before we were born.

This creates a psychological distortion.
You believe your timeline is your fault.
You believe your pace reflects your ability.
You believe your struggle is a sign of inadequacy.

It is none of those things.
It is the aftershock of inherited delay.

---

2. Comparison Magnifies the First-Gen Pressure

Most people compare themselves to their parents and feel behind.
First-generation Black wealth builders compare themselves to:

- friends from privileged backgrounds

- colleagues with financial backstops

- peers whose parents paid for school

- people who bought their first home with help

- people who never had debt

- people who never started from zero

- people who live without economic fear

This creates emotional distortion.

You may feel:

- slow when you are actually early

- behind when you are actually first

- inadequate when you are actually pioneering

- unaccomplished when you are actually historic for your lineage

Comparison takes your progress out of context.
And when context disappears, shame appears.

---

3. Social Media Turns Comparison Into a Weapon

Comparison is not new.
But social media industrialized it.

You can now observe:

- carefully curated lives

- staged success

- edited accomplishments

- invisible inheritance

- filtered lifestyles

- subtle performances

- artificial luxury

You scroll through thousands of reference points that are not real, not relevant, and not earned the way they appear.

Social media becomes a hall of mirrors.
You see yourself distorted by other people's projections.
You judge yourself through illusions.
You compare your reality to their performance.

You are not behind.
You are comparing your truth to their theater.

---

4. The Male Burden: Why Black Men Compare Themselves More Harshly

Black men are raised inside a performance trap:

- strength without vulnerability

- success without support

- leadership without guidance

- pressure without release

- responsibility without safety

In many communities, a Black man's value is tied to:

- income

- status

- stability

- protection

- provision

- achievement

So comparison hits harder because identity is tied to accomplishment.

Black boys grow into men who believe:

- success equals worth

- struggle equals failure

- asking for help equals weakness

- rest equals laziness

- uncertainty equals incompetence

- slow progress equals falling behind

This is not emotional fragility.
This is cultural conditioning.

Comparison becomes an attack on identity itself.

---

5. The Psychology: Why Comparison Hurts First-Gen Builders

Neuroscience shows that comparison activates the same regions of the brain triggered by social exclusion.

When you feel behind:

- your cortisol increases

- your anxiety heightens

- your self-perception shrinks

- your motivation destabilizes

- your decision-making worsens

This is intensified for first-generation Black builders because:

- you are carrying generational expectations

- you are breaking cycles in real time

- you are navigating spaces without mentors

- you are often the only one in the room

- you have no roadmap

- you feel like you must represent your entire family

- you cannot ask for help without fear of judgment

Comparison is not about envy.
Comparison is about pressure.

Your nervous system is reacting to a feeling of isolation in the climb.

---

6. The Trap: Measuring Yourself by Someone Else's Story

This is the moment you must understand something that ends the trap forever.

You were taught to measure yourself against timelines that were:

- built on inheritance

- built on access

- built on early compounding

- built on safety nets

- built on generational knowledge

- built on uninterrupted opportunity

You were not raised inside those conditions.
So your life is not supposed to look like theirs.
Your pace is not supposed to match theirs.
Your story is not supposed to mirror theirs.

You are not late.
You are building the foundation they were handed.

Your timeline is not flawed.
It is original.

---

7. The Escape: A New Measuring Stick

Comparison ends the moment you replace the wrong measuring stick with the right one.

Do not measure yourself by:

- age

- income

- titles

- followers

- home purchases

- job status

- family expectations

- social media illusions

Measure yourself by:

- stability you are creating

- cycles you are breaking

- knowledge you are gaining

- healing you are doing

- direction you are forming

- resilience you are showing

- clarity you are building

- opportunities you are opening for the next generation

You are not competing with other people's stories. You are creating the first chapter of your family's story.

You are the blueprint.
You are the beginning.
You are the reference point for those who come after you.

Comparison cannot exist when you realize you are the standard.

Chapter 8: The Myth of the Black Middle Class

Why It Looked Like Progress but Never Became Power

America loves the image of the Black middle class.
It celebrates it.
It studies it.
It markets it.
It uses it as proof of racial progress.

But the image was never the reality.

The Black middle class was built on:
income without assets,
success without safety,
stability without equity,
visibility without power,
education without inheritance.

It looked like progress.
It felt like progress.
It was progress.

But it was fragile from the beginning.

Because most of what we call the Black middle
class was not built on wealth.
It was built on work.

And work alone cannot create generational mobility.

This chapter explains why the Black middle class grew, why it never stabilized, and why the next generation must build differently.

Not out of shame.
Out of clarity.

---

1. The Rise: How the Black Middle Class Was Engineered

The Black middle class emerged after:
World War II economic shifts,
the GI Bill (from which Black veterans were widely excluded),
the Civil Rights movement,
government hiring expansions,
affirmative action policies,
industrial job openings,
expanding access to higher education.

But here is the truth:

Most early Black middle-class households were first-generation.

That means:
no inherited home,
no inherited savings,
no inherited stock,
no inherited business,
no inherited land.

Every advancement was brand new.
Every dollar was freshly earned.
Every step forward was unsupported.

The Black middle class was built by people who changed their income, not their lineage.

That is strength.
But it also creates vulnerability.

---

2. The Foundation Problem: Income Without Assets

The Black middle class was built on:
government jobs,
teaching positions,
nursing roles,
postal service work,
public administration,
military careers.

These were stable, honorable paths that created dignity and mobility.

But they did not create ownership.

Income is not wealth.
Status is not equity.
Degrees are not assets.
Titles are not protection.
Visibility is not financial insulation.

White middle-class families entered these same
eras with:
inherited homes,
inherited land,
inherited savings,
inherited stocks,
inherited business interests.

The starting lines were different.

So the outcomes were predictable.

---

3. The Trap: Lifestyle Over Leverage

Because Black middle-class families had no
inherited cushion, every step up felt fragile.

So what did many families do?

They protected their dignity by buying:
a nicer car,
nicer clothes,
nicer furniture,
a nicer home,
better schools for their kids.

This is not irresponsibility.
This is cultural survival.

Black dignity has always required presentation.
Respect was not given.
It had to be signaled.

But lifestyle spending did something unintended:

It consumed the dollars that should have become equity.

Parents provided stability for their children, but they could not provide financial momentum.

The next generation inherited:
love,
values,
strength,
discipline,
ambition,
pride.

But not assets.

That is the invisible trap.

---

4. The Fragility Problem: One Crisis Could Collapse Everything

White middle-class families often had a buffer.
If they lost a job, a parent stepped in.
If they needed a down payment, a grandparent helped.
If they had medical bills, someone had savings.
If tuition was due, someone wrote a check.

Black middle-class families often had no such cushion.

One unexpected downturn could collapse everything:
layoffs,
recessions,
health issues,
divorce,
a child's emergency,
a parent needing care.

What looked like middle class was often one hardship away from struggle.

This is not due to poor choices.
It is due to a lack of inherited insulation.

You cannot outwork fragility when fragility is structural.

---

5. The Psychological Pressure: Performing Prosperity

The Black middle class often felt forced to:
look successful,
sound successful,
dress successful,
behave successful.

Because:
we wanted to prove our worth,
we wanted to escape stereotypes,
we wanted our children to blend in,
we wanted distance from poverty,
we wanted safety in professionalism.

But performance distracted from strategy.

Black families mastered achievement.
We mastered excellence.
We mastered ambition.

But we did not receive the blueprint for:
tax advantages,
compounding,
business ownership,
lending systems,
equity accumulation,
strategic debt,
wealth psychology.

We perfected the presentation of success.
But we were denied the mechanics of wealth.

---

6. The Economic Truth: The Black Middle Class Was Never Allowed to Become Wealthy

Homeownership should have been the foundation of Black middle-class wealth.
But discriminatory policies weakened it.

Black families faced:
redlining,
higher interest rates,
predatory lending,
lower appraisals,
restricted neighborhoods,
undervalued homes,
fewer refinancing opportunities.

So even with the same education, the same income, the same house size, and the same work ethic, Black middle-class wealth grew slower.

This is not a community failure.
It is compounding inequality.

The rules were different.
And the outcomes reflect the rules.

6A. A Real Example: The 2008 Collapse Revealed the Truth

If you want proof that the Black middle class was built on fragile foundations, you do not have to look far.
All you have to do is look at 2008.

The housing collapse hit everyone, but it exposed the structural weakness inside Black middle-class wealth.
In places like Maryland, Virginia, and Washington, DC, many Black families were finally entering homeownership for the first time in history.

Prince George's (PG) County was the crown jewel.
It was the largest, most successful, most educated Black middle-class county in America.
It symbolized everything we were told to aim for:

good jobs,
good neighborhoods,
good schools,
safe communities,
respectable incomes,
stable mortgages.

But when the market collapsed, something devastating and revealing happened.

White neighborhoods in Montgomery County, Northern Virginia, and upper DC watched their home values drop and then recover within a few years.

But PG County became the national epicenter of Black wealth loss.

Black homeowners lost:
equity,
savings,
retirement buffers,
down payments,
neighborhoods,
stability.

Many saw their home values cut in half.
Some lost their homes entirely.
Some recovered only after a decade.
Some never recovered at all.

Why?

Because the Black middle class had income, but not insulation.

No inherited wealth.
No savings to absorb the shock.
No family assets to lean on.
No safety net.
No intergenerational cushion.
No backup capital.

So when the market shook, Black families fell farther and stayed down longer.

That collapse proved something painful:

The Black middle class was real.
Black middle-class wealth was not.

Income can vanish.
Equity takes decades to rebuild.
Generational wealth takes even longer.

The collapse revealed what the system knew all along:

Our progress was built on work, not assets.
Visibility, not power.
Homeownership, not true wealth.

It looked like we arrived.
But one downturn showed how fragile the foundation was.

The 2008 collapse also revealed a pattern in America rarely spoken aloud.

Black communities were often given the symbols of success without the structures of wealth.

Homeownership without equity.

Neighborhoods without insulation.

Status without safety nets.

PG County looked like an arrival, but one crisis proved the foundation was never allowed to be as strong as it appeared.

The system gave visibility, not power.

---

7. The Emotional Truth: The Middle Class Was Never Enough

The Black middle class was an achievement.
A breakthrough.
A miracle.
A triumph of resilience.

But it was never designed to become generational wealth.

It was dignity, not equity.
It was progress, not power.
It was visibility, not ownership.
It was mobility, not stability.
It was access, not autonomy.

And now you, the reader, are the one who must take the next step.

Not because the people before you failed.
But because they went as far as the system allowed them to go.

---

8. The New Path: Building What the Middle Class Could Not

Your parents and grandparents built:
safety,
education,
options,
upward mobility,
cultural pride.

Now it is your turn to build:
ownership,
equity,
freedom,
compounding,
long-term stability,
business infrastructure,
financial immunity.

Their ceiling becomes your floor.

This is not pressure.
This is opportunity.

Once you understand that the Black middle class was engineered to plateau, you also understand this:

You were never behind.
You were starting from the highest point your family ever reached.
Now you are responsible for the next level.

That is not a burden.
That is a blessing.

Chapter 9: The Myth of Black Spending Habits

Why the Story Was Never About Shopping, and What the Numbers Really Mean

There is a myth America loves to repeat.
A myth used in barbershops, classrooms, political speeches, and even corporate diversity meetings.

The myth says:
"Black people would be wealthy if they stopped buying shoes, clothes, cars, and jewelry."

It is a convenient lie.
A lie that blames the community instead of the system.
A lie that distracts from structural inequality by pointing at individual behavior.
A lie that shames Black culture for expressing itself in the only ways available.

This chapter dismantles the myth completely.

Because Black America does not have a spending problem.
Black America has a **starting-line problem**, a **structural problem**, and a **wealth-access problem**.

And the data proves it.

---

1. The Myth Was Designed to Mislead You

The spending myth did not come from research.
It came from stereotypes.

It came from the same place that manufactured the idea that:

- Black people are irresponsible

- Black people lack discipline

- Black people prefer consumption over investment

- Black culture is financially immature

- Black communities mismanage money

These claims were not built on facts.
They were built on racist assumptions used to justify inequality.

Because the moment you convince a community that its failure is cultural, you no longer have to explain the **structural forces** that created the gap.

The myth shifts attention away from:

- redlining

- predatory lending

- wage discrimination

- hiring bias

- violent destruction of Black wealth

- unequal school funding

- restricted investment access

- lack of intergenerational assets

- suppressed home appraisals

- the wealth tax of being Black

The spending myth protects the system by blaming its victims.

---

2. The Numbers Tell the Truth: Black People Spend Less Than the Myth Claims

Whenever the spending myth is repeated, people assume it is backed by research.
It isn't.

Federal Bureau of Labor Statistics data shows clearly:

Black households spend **less** on:

- Housing (in proportion to income)

- Food

- Healthcare

- Education

- Insurance

- Retirement contributions

- Investments

And slightly **more** on:

- Transportation

- Apparel

- Personal care

These differences are not because of irresponsibility. They are because of **circumstance**.

Communities with long commutes spend more on transportation.

Communities targeted by predatory auto lending spend more on cars.
Communities denied wealth signals use fashion as visibility.
Communities with less safety invest more in presentation.

None of this explains the wealth gap.

Because the wealth gap was created **before Black spending began**.

---

3. The Real Equation: You Cannot Spend Your Way Out of Structural Inequality

Wealth is created by:

- inheritance

- investment access

- early homeownership

- compounding over decades

- business ownership

- asset appreciation

- tax advantages

- family transfers

- low-interest borrowing

- safety nets

Black families were locked out of all of these for 90 percent of American history.

The average white family's wealth is not due to spending less.
It is because they **inherited more**.

The average Black family's lack of wealth is not due to irresponsible spending.
It is because they **started with nothing**.

You cannot discipline your way out of generational deprivation.
You cannot budget your way into inheritance.
You cannot coupon your way into compounding.
You cannot "stop buying shoes" your way into a trust fund.
You cannot live frugally your way into 400 years of missed ownership.

Money grows through assets, not restraint.

And the assets were never given equally.

4. The Psychology Behind the Myth: Shame as Control

The spending myth creates internalized shame.
It convinces Black people that poverty is personal failure.
It convinces Black families that they are the problem.
It convinces Black children that wealth is about behavior, not history.
It convinces the world that inequality is cultural, not constructed.

Shame turns injustice into a personal flaw.
Shame turns systemic oppression into a moral conversation.
Shame makes the oppressed carry the emotional burden of the oppressor.

This is why the myth survives.

Because if Black people believe they are the cause, they will never question the structure.

They will never demand access.
They will never demand capital.
They will never demand equity.
They will never demand repair.

Shame is the quietest tool of oppression.

5. The Historical Truth: Black Spending Was Always Monitored

You cannot understand the myth without understanding the past.

Throughout American history, Black economic behavior was:

- controlled

- restricted

- criminalized

- surveilled

- manipulated

- economically punished

After slavery, laws were passed to keep Black people from displaying any form of prosperity.
During Jim Crow, Black financial activity was tracked to limit advancement.
In the 20th century, Black neighborhoods were targeted by high-cost lenders to extract wealth.
Fashion and style became expressions of dignity in a world that denied it.

So when Black people dressed well, it was not vanity.

It was resistance.
It was pride.
It was survival.
It was the right to appear human in a society that tried to erase humanity.

The myth misreads this survival as irresponsibility.

---

6. The Real Spending Problem: America, Not Black America

If overspending were the cause of the wealth gap, then white Americans would be just as poor.

But they are not.

Because the gap is not created by:

- daily purchases

- clothing

- cars

- shoes

- meals

- entertainment

The gap is created by:

- unequal access to investment vehicles

- unequal access to capital

- unequal access to home appreciation

- unequal access to family money

- unequal access to cheap credit

- unequal access to tax advantages

- unequal access to inheritance

- unequal access to safe communities

- unequal access to financial protection

This has nothing to do with spending.
This is about **structural economic design**.

---

7. The Trap: Using Individual Behavior to Hide Institutional Responsibility

The spending myth is used to silence the real conversation.

Because if society admits the truth, it must also admit responsibility:

- for stolen land

- for stolen labor

- for broken promises

- for discriminatory institutions

- for one-sided policies

- for centuries of economic exclusion

The myth protects the status quo by shifting focus to shoes instead of systems.

You cannot fix inequality by blaming choices made inside inequality.

---

8. The Liberation: Understanding What Actually Builds Wealth

The moment you understand that spending habits are not the cause of the wealth gap, everything changes.

Because wealth comes from:

- ownership

- access

- exposure

- early literacy

- equity appreciation

- institutional protection

- low-interest capital

- compounding

- inheritance

- networks

- community infrastructure

The foundation of Black America was denied.

Your path forward is not about guilt.
It is about awareness.

It is about replacing myths with mechanics.
It is about replacing shame with strategy.
It is about replacing stereotypes with systems.
It is about replacing cultural criticism with structural understanding.

You do not escape poverty by restricting your joy.
You escape by increasing your ownership.

And that is where we go next.

Chapter 10: The Golden Children Myth

Why Our Success Was Never Proof of Equality

America loves the idea of the exceptional Black individual.
The standout.
The prodigy.
The overachiever.
The one who "made it out."
The one who proves that anything is possible.

The Golden Child.

You know who they are.
Maybe you were one.
Maybe you raised one.
Maybe you carried the weight of being one.

The Golden Child Myth is the belief that a few successful Black individuals represent upward mobility for the entire community.
That their success proves that generational barriers no longer matter.
That their achievements cancel out structural inequality.

But the Golden Child was never evidence of equality.
The Golden Child was evidence of **exception**.

This chapter explains the psychological, cultural, and economic consequences of a myth created to celebrate Black excellence while ignoring Black reality.

---

1. The Golden Child Is a Product of Survival, Not Equality

For decades, many Black families poured everything into one child.
Not because they wanted favorites.
Not because they believed only one child deserved to succeed.
But because resources were limited and hope was fragile, families invested in the child who::

- followed the rules,

- showed discipline,

- excelled academically,

- stayed focused,

- avoided danger,

- carried family dreams with maturity beyond their age.

This child often became:

- the first to graduate,

- the first to travel,

- the first to get a salary job,

- the first to enter a professional career,

- the first to buy a home,

- the first to "make it out."

But this rise was not proof of equality.

It was proof of sacrifice.

The Golden Child was a miracle produced under pressure.

---

2. The Pressure: Excellence as a Form of Emotional Survival

The Golden Child grows up with unspoken expectations:

- do not fail

- do not embarrass us

- do not go backwards

- do not waste opportunities

- do not stop achieving

- do not become the story we fear

Pressure becomes identity.

The Golden Child learns that:

- love is tied to performance

- safety comes from being exceptional

- family pride depends on their achievements

- they must mature faster than their peers

- rest is dangerous

- mistakes are unacceptable

- vulnerability is a luxury they cannot afford

This is not encouragement.
This is survival.

And survival disguised as motivation becomes emotional debt.

---

3. The System's Role: Celebrating the Exception to Hide the Rule

America loves exceptional Black individuals because they allow the system to avoid accountability.

The Golden Child becomes:

- the diversity example,

- the corporate mascot,

- the scholarship story,

- the hiring brochure,

- the inspirational speaker,

- the symbol of "progress."

The message becomes:
"If they can do it, why can't the rest?"

But this is psychological manipulation.

You cannot justify structural inequality with an anecdote.

A single success story does not erase:

- redlining

- underfunded schools

- generational poverty

- discriminatory hiring

- unequal inheritance

- biased policing

- predatory lending

- suppressed wages

- historical exclusion

The Golden Child is not proof that the playing field is fair.
They are proof of what happens when one person outruns barriers others never had.

---

4. The Economic Truth: Golden Children Built Income, Not Wealth

Most Golden Children:

- got degrees

- got good jobs

- entered professional spaces their families never accessed

- bought homes

- became financially stable

- supported parents or siblings

- carried the family forward

But here is what rarely happened:

They did not inherit wealth.
They did not receive down payments.
They did not receive trusts.
They did not receive businesses.
They did not receive market exposure as children.
They did not receive financial runway.
They did not receive generational insulation.

They succeeded despite the lack of infrastructure, not because they had it.

Their success was built on:

- exhaustion

- discipline

- constant self-correction

- perfectionism

- pressure

- early responsibility

- fear of letting people down

They climbed without a ladder.

That is resilience.
It is not equality.

---

5. The Emotional Cost: Isolation at the Top

Golden Children often live with:

- survivor's guilt

- fear of falling

- anxiety around maintaining status

- pressure to take care of others

- loneliness in professional spaces

- no margin for personal mistakes

- burnout disguised as ambition

They become:

- the problem solver,

- the financial buffer,

- the emotional anchor,

- the one everyone calls,

- the one who handles everything.

But who handles them?

This is the emotional truth America ignores:

The Golden Child is celebrated publicly and burdened privately.

The world praises them.
But few understand them.

---

6. The Myth Hurts the Entire Community

The Golden Child Myth does not only burden individuals.
It damages collective progress.

It creates:

- unrealistic expectations

- unfair comparisons

- resentment within families

- pressure on younger siblings

- distorted ideas of success

- emotional distance

- silence around struggle

- shame around setbacks

It also convinces society that:

- racism is over,

- hard work solves everything,

- opportunity is equal,

- inequality is cultural.

The myth is not just a misunderstanding.
It is a tool.

It hides the system behind the individual.

---

7. The Truth: There Were Never Golden Children. Only Golden Expectations.

The Golden Child was not chosen.
They were needed.

They became the proof that the family had hope.
The proof that sacrifice was worth it.
The proof that potential could survive pressure.
The proof that progress was possible.

But here is the truth the myth never admits:

Golden Children were never golden.
They were early.

They were the first to climb a mountain that other families had been scaling for generations.

Their success was not a sign that Black families had caught up.
It was a sign that Black families were still climbing.

---

8. The Liberation: Success Without the Burden of Symbolism

The next generation must redefine success.

To free Golden Children from:

- unrealistic responsibility

- burnout

- emotional exhaustion

- guilt

- fear of disappointing

- constant self-repair

And to free families from:

- comparing children

- choosing one "hope"

- linking love to achievement

- tying identity to performance

True generational wealth is built when:

- achievement becomes shared,

- knowledge becomes shared,

- pressure becomes shared,

- assets become shared.

The goal is not to produce more Golden Children.
The goal is to produce stable families.

The next era of Black wealth is not about
exceptional individuals.
It is about collective elevation.

It is no longer about the one who "made it out."
It is about entire families rising together.

And for the first time in history, that is possible.

Because now you understand the myth.
You are free from it.
You are no longer the exception.
You are the beginning of the infrastructure that
your family never had.

Chapter 11: The Black Wall Street Blueprint

What We Built Before They Burned It

Before we talk about what is possible for Black first-generation wealth builders today, you must understand something that history often tries to bury:

We already built it.
We built it before Wall Street acknowledged us.
We built it before corporate America hired us.
We built it before the country believed we could.

And we built it at a time when everything was designed to stop us.

Tulsa was not a miracle.
It was a blueprint.

---

1. Black Wall Street Was Not A Fairy Tale. It Was An Economic Ecosystem.

Many people talk about Black Wall Street as if it were a myth.
A story told with pride but detached from practicality.

But the truth is simple:

Greenwood was one of the most sophisticated, self-sustaining Black economic ecosystems in American history.

Not symbolic success.
Real success.
Measured in institutions, not inspiration.

Tulsa had:

- banks

- insurance companies

- schools

- newspapers

- hospitals

- law offices

- real estate developers

- grocery stores

- taxi services

- transportation systems

- upscale hotels

- restaurants

- retail shops

- libraries

- thriving churches

- investment clubs

- business associations

This was not representation.
This was infrastructure.

Greenwood was not just "Black business."
It was Black ownership.
Black leadership.
Black capital circulation.
Black economic protection.
Black communal advancement.

Tulsa was not a dream.
It was documentation.

---

2. What They Built And Why It Worked

The power of Greenwood was not in what they sold.
It was in how the community functioned.

They understood the four laws of wealth long before economists articulated them.

Law 1: Circulation Over Consumption

A dollar in Greenwood circulated **36 times** before leaving the community.

Most American communities today see circulation of just **2–3 times**.

Greenwood showed the power of economic recycling, where money does not leak out; it multiplies inward.

Law 2: Ownership Over Access

They did not just open businesses.
They owned the land, the buildings, the infrastructure.

They were landlords, lenders, developers, brokers, investors.

Ownership is what builds generational wealth.
And Greenwood understood this without textbooks or MBAs.

Law 3: Education Over Status

Schools in Greenwood were elite.

Children learned:

- business

- finance

- literature

- etiquette

- trades

- leadership

- professionalism

Education was not symbolic.
It was strategic.

And unlike segregated white schools, Black schools in Greenwood produced thinkers and entrepreneurs at scale.

Law 4: Community Over Individualism

One person did not build black Wall Street.

It was collective:

- collective risk

- collective protection

- collective advancement

- collective vision

- collective responsibility

Wealth was not a competition.
It was a shared mission.

This is the opposite of the Golden Child myth.

Greenwood proved a truth America feared:

Black wealth is most powerful when it is shared.

---

3. Why The System Saw It As A Threat

People often say Tulsa was burned because of a false accusation.

That was the spark.
Not the cause.

The real threat was **Black prosperity**.

Greenwood proved:

- Black people could run banks

- Black people could manage real estate

- Black people could create thriving economies

- Black people could out-earn white communities

- Black business districts could outperform white districts

- Black investors were capable of building asset-based wealth

- Black children could be better educated than white children

This was not allowed to stand.

Because Greenwood shattered every stereotype America used to justify inequality.

Greenwood proved that the problem was never Black ability.

The problem was Black possibility.

And when possibility becomes power, systems get nervous.

---

4. Destruction Was Not Spontaneous. It Was Strategic.

The Tulsa massacre of 1921 was not simply mob violence.
It was an orchestrated economic attack.

Over:

- 1,200 homes burned

- 600 businesses destroyed

- 10,000 Black residents displaced

- Millions of dollars in property erased

- Generational wealth wiped out

- Insurance claims denied

- Land stolen

- Prosperity criminalized

The goal was not chaos.
The goal was disruption.

Destroy the infrastructure.
Destroy the future.
Destroy the proof of what Black people can build.

And yet, despite the destruction, here's what they did not destroy:

The blueprint.

---

5. What Tulsa Proves About Black Wealth

Tulsa is not just history.
It is evidence.

Evidence that the narrative about Black spending is false.
Evidence that Black communities can build investment ecosystems.
Evidence that Black entrepreneurship is not new.
Evidence that Black excellence is structural, not symbolic.
Evidence that Black advancement is possible without assimilation.
Evidence that Black wealth was always achievable.

Tulsa is proof that when Black people have:

- safety

- land

- ownership

- capital

- community

- literacy

- leadership

- strategy

We build faster, smarter, and more creatively than the country expects.

Tulsa is not just a wound.
It is a warning.
And a roadmap.

---

6. The Blueprint We Lost; And Must Rebuild

The blueprint of Black Wall Street reveals five principles that still apply today.

Principle 1: Build Locally, Leverage Globally

Greenwood did not wait for permission.
They built with what they had, then scaled beyond it.

Principle 2: Community Is the Original Venture Capital

Black families were each other's investors.

Before banks allowed loans, the community funded itself.

Principle 3: Ownership Must Come Before Recognition

Greenwood did not chase visibility.
They chased assets.

Principle 4: Economic Protection Is Cultural Protection

Wealth protected the community from exploitation.
It gave Black families options and safety.

Principle 5: Institutions Matter More Than Individuals

There was no Golden Child.
There was a Golden Community.

The future of Black wealth depends on returning to these principles, in modern forms.

---

7. Interrupted, Not Erased

Tulsa is not just a story of destruction.
It is a story of interruption.

An explosion can destroy buildings.
But it cannot destroy intelligence.
It cannot destroy culture.
It cannot destroy strategy.
It cannot destroy capacity.
It cannot destroy the blueprint.

The blueprint survived because it was never written on paper.
It was written in us.

And now, a century later, the blueprint is being rewritten:

- in tech

- in real estate

- in media

- in decentralized finance

- in online entrepreneurship

- in digital communities

- in education

- in ownership models

- in intergenerational planning

The spirit of Greenwood never left.
It simply needed a generation with enough clarity to rebuild it.

That generation is you.

---

8. The New Black Wall Street Will Not Look Like the Old One

We do not need to recreate Greenwood exactly.
We need to recreate its function.

Today, Black wealth can grow through:

- digital ownership

- content-based business models

- online education

- intellectual property

- group economics

- investment clubs

- real estate syndication

- tech startups

- cooperative models

- brand ownership

- media platforms

- AI-enabled businesses

- decentralized networks

The next Black Wall Street will not be a
neighborhood.
It will be a system.
A network.
A culture.
A structure built across cities, industries, and digital
spaces.

The blueprint did not die.
It evolved.

---

9. The Lesson: There Was Never a Lack of Ability. Only a Lack of Allowance.

Tulsa proves a truth this book has repeated from every angle:

You are not behind.
You were held back.
Your community was held back.
Your lineage was held back.
Your potential was held back.

But the ability?
The intelligence?
The innovation?
The creativity?
The leadership?
The economic talent?

That was always there.

Greenwood is the proof.

And now you have the chance to build without interruption.

This time, not as a miracle.
As a movement.

Chapter 12: The Illusion of Black Wealth

Athletes, Entertainers, and the Misleading Story America Loves

There is a story America loves to tell about Black success.
The story says we made it.
The story says we are wealthy.
The story says racism is over because:

- athletes sign million-dollar contracts

- entertainers sell out arenas

- rappers buy homes in the hills

- celebrities drive exotic cars

- Black culture dominates global entertainment

This story is comforting.
This story is convenient.
And this story is false.

Because the truth is simple:

Black fame is not Black wealth.
Black visibility is not Black ownership.

Black excellence in entertainment does not translate into Black economic power.

And the numbers prove it.

---

1. Why America Loves This Myth

The myth serves a purpose.

It allows people to believe:

- the playing field is fair

- talent solves inequality

- success is accessible to all

- the system works

- Black exceptionalism is normal

In reality:

- there are 30,000 Black doctors

- 60,000 Black engineers

- hundreds of thousands of Black accountants, teachers, managers, lawyers

- millions of Black workers in everyday professions

Yet society points to:

- 450 NBA players

- 1,700 NFL players

- a few hundred celebrities

- a handful of megastars

And pretends this is the representative picture of Black success.

It is not.

Those people are the statistical outliers of outliers.

The myth survives because it makes the system feel innocent.

---

2. The Entertainment Path Was Not Chosen. It Was Allowed.

For over a century, Black people were pushed into fields that offered:

- visibility

- entertainment

- physical labor

- emotional performance

- service roles

Not power.
Not ownership.
Not infrastructure.

Black excellence in:

- music

- sports

- comedy

- dance

- acting

was embraced long before Black excellence in:

- banking

- real estate

- medicine

- law

- engineering

- technology

- investing

- politics

- corporate leadership

Entertainment was one of the only lanes where society permitted Black brilliance to shine.

They allowed our fame, because fame does not create power.
They restricted our ownership, because ownership does.

Fame entertains the country.
Ownership changes the country.

Fame makes people visible.
Ownership makes people influential.

Fame is celebrated.
Ownership is protected.

Fame fills arenas.
Ownership fills bank accounts.

Fame creates fans.
Ownership creates futures.

Black excellence was allowed in the spotlight.
Black power was denied behind the scenes.

That is the difference between expression and infrastructure.
And that difference shaped the entire trajectory of Black wealth in America.

---

3. Visibility Is Not Wealth

When people see Black celebrities, they assume wealth is common.

But Black celebrity wealth exists in a world where:

- most Black families have **zero** assets

- Black home appraisals are suppressed

- Black students carry the highest student loan burdens

- Black businesses receive the least bank financing

- Black workers earn less, even with the same degree

- Black families inherit one-tenth of what white families inherit

Visibility creates illusion.
It does not create wealth.

The same society that sees a Black athlete sign a $100 million contract often does not see:

- the lack of generational assets behind him

- the lack of financial literacy he was taught

- the financial responsibilities placed on him by family

- the taxes that cut the contract in half

- the career length that averages 3.3 years

- the predatory advisors that target him

- the emotional pressure of being "the one"

A black celebrity makes success look normal.
But it is the opposite.

It is rare, fragile, and often unsustained.

---

4. The Jewish Phenomenon Comparison Matters

One of the most important lessons from *The Jewish Phenomenon* is this:

Wealth in Jewish communities is not built through extraordinary careers.
It is built through ordinary professions practiced at scale.

Doctors.
Lawyers.
Accountants.
Teachers.
Entrepreneurs.
Small business owners.
Investors.
Managers.
Engineers.
Consultants.

Stable, respected, transferable professions that:

- produce consistent income

- build assets

- create intergenerational stability

- pass down knowledge

- plug into investment networks

- reinforce literacy

- compound over decades

Black America was never allowed to build wealth this way.

Our visibility is high.
Our access is low.

Their power is quiet.
Our success is loud.

They build through institutions.
We are celebrated through performance.

Their wealth is engineered.
Our wealth is displayed.

And displays fade long before institutions fall.

---

5. When Fame Becomes the Only Blueprint

When kids grow up seeing only athletes, entertainers, rappers, influencers, and performers at the top, something dangerous happens.

They believe:

- success requires talent, not strategy

- wealth is earned publicly, not quietly

- influence matters more than ownership

- entertainment is the primary path

- visibility equals value

- celebrity equals wealth

This miseducation narrows ambition.

Because a child cannot aspire to what they do not see.

And when Black children are only shown limelight careers...
while white, Jewish, and Asian children are shown wealth pathways.....
the gap widens at the blueprint level.

Not because of culture.
Because of exposure.

---

6. The Real Math: Celebrity Wealth Cannot Lift A Community

Even if every current Black athlete and entertainer became billionaires, it would not close the wealth gap.

Why?

Because their numbers are too small.

Their industries are too unpredictable.

Their careers are too short.

Their wealth is too concentrated.

And the money does not become community infrastructure.

Athlete wealth is income-rich and asset-unstable.

An entertainer wealth is market-dependent.

Celebrity wealth is:

- high-visibility

- high-risk

- high-consumption

- low-intergenerational transfer rates

- low community reinvestment

It is not the foundation of generational wealth.

The Jewish, Lebanese, Korean, Indian, Nigerian, and Chinese communities did not build generational power through celebrity.

They built it through ordinary excellence.

---

7. The Psychological Damage of the Comparison

Black adults grow up comparing their progress to outliers.

Not to regular white peers with:

- two-parent assets

- home equity

- business inheritance

- college savings

- trust fund buffers

But to:

- Beyoncé

- LeBron

- Rihanna

- Diddy

- Drake

- influencers

- celebrities

- entertainers

Comparing your life to someone whose *job is visibility* distorts reality.

It makes achievement feel small.
It makes progress feel slow.
It makes wealth feel impossible.
It makes stability feel inadequate.
It makes you feel behind in a race you were not even running.

8. The Truth: Black Wealth Will Not Be Built by Outliers

Black generational wealth will be built by:

- engineers

- doctors

- lawyers

- nurses

- real estate investors

- teachers

- accountants

- small business owners

- entrepreneurs

- software developers

- therapists

- construction owners

- electricians

- consultants

- investors

- tradespeople

- managers

- professionals of all kinds

Ordinary people building extraordinary stability.

This is how other communities do it.
This is how Black communities will do it.

Your wealth will not come from standing out.
It will come from compounding.

Your future will not be built by applause.
It will be built by ownership.

Your family's legacy will not come from entertainment.
It will come from structure.

We do not need more stars.
We need more systems.

---

9. The Lesson: Fame Is Not a Solution. Ownership Is.

This chapter is not an attack on entertainers.
It is an adjustment of perspective.

We honor our artists.
We celebrate our athletes.
We respect our talent.

But the future of Black wealth will not come from individuals in the spotlight.

It will come from communities in formation.

Fame is unstable.
Ownership is generational.

Visibility fades.
Equity grows.

The spotlight moves.
Assets remain.

The world may celebrate Black brilliance on stage.

But the next era of Black wealth will happen off stage.

Quietly.
Strategically.
Consistently.
Collectively.

History shows that when we stop chasing visibility and start building infrastructure, everything changes.

And now, for the first time in centuries, the infrastructure is within reach.

Chapter 13: The Now Advantage

Why This Is the Best Time in History to Be a First-Generation Black Wealth Builder

For most of American history, the game was not fair.
The rules were not equal.
The opportunities were not available.
The doors were not open.

You were not behind.
You were blocked.

But something happened in the last twenty years.
Quietly.
Gradually.
Irreversibly.

The old systems that controlled access, land, schooling, capital, gatekeepers, and institutions weakened.
And new systems emerged that reward:

- creativity

- consistency

- ownership

- digital presence

- skill-building

- entrepreneurship

- visibility

- information access

The Now Advantage is simple:

You are the first generation with access to tools that do not care about race, background, neighborhood, inheritance, or gatekeepers.

But to see the advantage, you must finally see the shift.

---

1. Access Has Collapsed

For centuries, Black progress was blocked by:

- banks

- schools

- unions

- licensing boards

- neighborhoods

- real estate markets

- education systems

- employment networks

- capital providers

- cultural gatekeepers

Today, many of those doors have cracked open — not because of morality, but because of technology.

Access has collapsed.

You can:

- learn any skill online

- publish content without permission

- build a brand without pedigree

- sell products without inventory

- raise money without banks

- start businesses with minimal cash

- connect with global markets

- turn knowledge into income

- reach audiences directly

- build platforms from scratch

- create assets with AI

The world that blocked you no longer has the same control.

Access has been decentralized.

---

2. Gatekeepers Have Lost Their Power

In the old world:

- industries decided who succeeded

- corporations decided who was worthy

- institutions decided who was credible

- publishers decided who could speak

- universities decided who was educated

- employers decided who was valuable

That world is disappearing.

Today:

- YouTube is bigger than major broadcasters

- Shopify is bigger than retail gatekeepers

- TikTok is bigger than Hollywood marketing

- Substack is bigger than many newsrooms

- AI lets anyone produce professional-level work

- creators earn more than many employees

- digital businesses scale faster than traditional ones

You do not need permission to build.

And the people who once controlled opportunity can no longer stop you.

This is unprecedented.

3. The Rise of Digital Ownership

For the first time, Black wealth can be built in ways that require:

- no capital

- no real estate

- no gatekeepers

- no inheritance

- no approvals

Digital ownership changes everything.

You can own:

- content

- courses

- communities

- IP

- software

- digital products

- media

- brand assets

- online stores

- AI-generated creations

- licensing rights

- distribution channels

Your grandparents had to buy land to own something.
Your parents had to get a degree to achieve stability.
You can seize an opportunity with a laptop and discipline.

This is power the system cannot block.

---

4. The Information Gap Has Closed

For the first time in Black history:

- financial literacy is everywhere

- business education is accessible

- investing is no longer elite

- mentorship is online

- information is democratized

- knowledge is on demand

- the blueprint is open-source

You no longer need:

- a wealthy parent

- a mentor in-house

- a professional network

- access to elite circles

- private education

The information that was once hidden is now free.

This is the collapse of the Miseducation Machine.

---

5. The Cost to Start Has Dropped to Nearly Zero

In the old economy, wealth required:

- capital

- inventory

- equipment

- retail space

- corporate sponsorship

- business loans

- proximity to opportunity

This generation can start with:

- a phone

- an internet connection

- free software

- low-cost tools

- digital distribution

- AI assistance

- online platforms

The most significant shift in wealth creation today is not skill.

It is **cost reduction**.

When the cost to start falls, opportunity rises.

---

6. The Return on Skill Is Higher Than Ever

Historically:

- land was wealth

- equipment was wealth

- capital was wealth

- real estate was wealth

- labor was wealth

Today:

- **skill is wealth**

- creativity is wealth

- brand is wealth

- attention is wealth

- intellect is wealth

- execution is wealth

- digital leverage is wealth

This shift favors those who:

- learn quickly

- adapt fast

- stay curious

- take initiative

- create consistently

This generation will be paid for what they can produce, not what they were born with.

This is the opposite of old wealth.

---

7. The First-Generation Advantage

If you grew up without wealth, you developed:

- resilience

- creativity

- improvisation

- resourcefulness

- problem-solving

- grit

- emotional endurance

- hunger

- adaptability

These traits were survival before.
Now they are currency.

You are built for the new economy because you had no other choice.

And what was once a disadvantage, starting late, starting alone, starting without a map, becomes an advantage in a world where:

- the rules change fast

- stability is temporary

- adaptation is vital

- creativity wins

- grit outperforms entitlement

The world now rewards exactly what your life produced.

---

8. Why This Matters

Because the book has been telling you:

You were not behind.
You were never given the map.

Chapter 13 tells you something new:

Now the map is public.
Now the tools are available.
Now the gatekeepers are weak.
Now the cost to start is low.
Now the world rewards your strengths.

This is the moment the playing field does not tilt in your favor...
but it is no longer tilted against you.

And for the first time in centuries, that is enough.

Chapter 14: The Wealth Traps to Avoid

The Pitfalls That Keep First-Generation Black Builders From Moving Forward

Most wealth books focus on what to do.
But just as important, sometimes more important, is learning what to avoid.

Because being a first-generation Black wealth builder means you are:

- learning in real time

- building without guidance

- navigating systems not designed for you

- correcting generational gaps

- creating stability from scratch

- carrying emotional and financial burdens at once

This chapter is about protecting your progress.

Because wealth is not only built by making good decisions.
Wealth is preserved by avoiding destructive ones.

These are the traps that quietly drain Black first-generation builders every day.

---

1. The Income Trap

Confusing high income with wealth

You can earn 150,000 and be broke.
You can earn 60,000 and be wealthy.

Income is not wealth.
Lifestyle is not wealth.
Appearances are not wealth.

Only ownership creates wealth.

The trap occurs when:

- income rises faster than discipline

- lifestyle expands faster than assets

- consumption grows faster than investments

- visibility replaces structure

Black professionals often fall into this trap because:

- we were raised with scarcity

- we want to live better now

- we want to reward ourselves

- we want to appear successful

- our family expects support

- we never saw wealth modeled

The solution:

Treat income like fuel, not proof.
Convert income into assets before lifestyle.

---

2. The Survival Obligations Trap

Being the family safety net without building your own foundation

First-generation builders often feel responsible for:

- parents

- siblings

- cousins

- extended family

- emergencies

- unexpected bills

- financial crises

Love is not the problem.
Lack of boundaries is.

This trap delays wealth because you cannot build for tomorrow if every crisis pulls you back into yesterday.

The solution:

Set a support budget.
Not from guilt, from structure.
You cannot save everyone while staying financially fragile yourself.

---

3. The Debt Illusion Trap

Using debt to create the appearance of stability

Debt is marketed as access.
Sometimes it is.
Often it is not.

The trap begins when:

- loans replace savings

- credit replaces planning

- financing replaces patience

- leases replace ownership

- student loans replace strategy

Black borrowers are targeted heavily:

- higher interest rates

- predatory lending

- inflated appraisals

- aggressive marketing

- limited financial literacy sources

- limited inherited safety nets

Debt becomes normal.
Debt becomes expected.
Debt becomes invisible.

The solution:

Use debt only to buy time or build assets, never to maintain image.

---

4. The Comparison Trap (Revisited)

Measuring progress against people who started miles ahead

The fastest way to lose financial direction is to:

- compare your home to someone with inherited equity

- compare your pace to someone with a safety net

- compare your career to someone with insider access

- compare your car to someone with family money

- compare your progress to someone who never had student loans

Comparison triggers:

- financial anxiety

- unnecessary spending

- rushing decisions

- shame-driven purchases

- emotional overspending

The solution:

Compare your life only to your starting line, not someone else's inheritance.

---

5. The Delayed Investing Trap

Waiting for the right time to invest

First-generation builders often:

- fear losing money

- distrust financial markets

- feel late

- feel unprepared

- grew up in unstable financial environments

This trap is deadly because:

- inflation punishes saving

- time multiplies money more than income does

- delaying investing delays freedom

- you cannot catch up later

The solution:

Invest small, early, and consistently.
The amount matters less than the repetition.

---

6. The Do It Alone Trap

Trying to build wealth without community, mentors, or networks

This trap comes from:

- pride

- survival mode

- being the first

- lack of trust

- being used to doing everything alone

- not wanting to appear ignorant

But wealth is a team sport.

No community in the world built wealth through individual success.

The solution:

Build a circle.
Join groups.
Find mentors.
Seek models.
Ask questions.
Use community leverage.

You cannot build generational wealth in isolation.

---

7. The No Blueprint Trap

Building without structure, systems, or a plan

Many first-generation builders:

- save sporadically

- invest irregularly

- lack a long-term wealth plan

- have unclear goals

- do not track net worth

- mix business and personal finances

- hope instead of plan

- react instead of design

This keeps wealth fragile.

The solution:

Treat your wealth like a business.
Systems create stability.
Stability creates options.

---

8. The Lifestyle Creep Trap

Expanding spending every time income rises

Every raise becomes:

- a new car

- a nicer apartment

- more subscriptions

- more eating out

- more gifts

- more upgrades

- more convenience spending

Lifestyle creep destroys wealth in silence.

Because you never feel rich, just comfortable and stuck.

The solution:

When income goes up, savings and investing should go up first.
Lifestyle later. Maybe.

---

9. The I Will Start Later Trap

Believing time will wait for you

This is the most dangerous trap of all.

The belief that you have:

- more time

- more energy

- more room to figure it out

- more space to plan later

You do not.

Generational wealth is built by:

- starting small

- starting messy

- starting uncertain

- starting early

And then letting time do what hustle cannot.

The solution:

Start now.
Adjust later.
Grow forever.

---

10. The Trap of Silence

Avoiding money conversations out of shame, pride, or protection

Black families historically avoided money talk because:

- we had none

- it triggered pain

- it created conflict

- it revealed inequality

- it exposed vulnerability

- it reminded us of lack

But silence is expensive.

Families without financial communication:

- repeat mistakes

- pass down fear

- fail to transfer knowledge

- hide debt

- misunderstand income

- never prepare the next generation

- stay in the dark

The solution:

Talk about money.
Normalize it.
Teach it.
Share what you learn.

Silence protects nothing.
Knowledge protects everything.

The Lesson of Chapter 14

You cannot build the future if you fall into the traps that destroyed the past.

This chapter is not about fear.
It is about precision.

You already know what blocked your ancestors.
Now you know what can block you.

The next chapters will show you exactly how to build forward, clearly, confidently, and structurally.

Chapter 15: The Real Black Middle Class

Why Income Looks Similar, but Wealth Does Not

In America, "middle class" is a label used loosely.
It is tied to:

- salary

- neighborhood

- education

- job title

- lifestyle

- social circles

But those measurements hide a deeper truth.

A Black family earning 90,000 a year is not the same as a white or Asian family earning 90,000 dollars a year.

A Black homeowner in a nice neighborhood is not the same as a white homeowner in that same neighborhood.

A Black professional with a degree is not the same as a white professional with a degree.

Not because of intelligence.
Not because of culture.
Not because of effort.

Because of **structure**.

The American middle class was built on wealth, not income.
But Black families were given income long before they were allowed to access wealth.

This chapter explains the difference.

---

1. The Black Middle Class Was Built by Education, Not Assets

After the civil rights movement, Black progress came primarily through:

- college degrees

- government jobs

- union jobs

- nursing

- teaching

- civil service

- military careers

- administrative roles

These were stable, respectable, important careers.
They created income.
They created mobility.

But they did not create wealth.

Why?

Because wealth comes from:

- home appreciation

- inheritance

- business ownership

- stock portfolios

- investments

- land

- trusts

- compounding assets

Black families were not given access to these until very recently, and often with structural limitations.

So the Black middle class became:

income-rich and asset-light.

This is the foundation of the gap.

---

2. The Illusion of Parity

On the surface, Black middle-class life looks similar to others:

- college degree

- job with benefits

- homeownership

- suburban neighborhood

- two cars

- kids in sports or activities

But when you look deeper:

- white families pass down home equity

- Asian families transfer business assets

- Jewish families transfer financial portfolios

- Indian and Middle Eastern families transfer education and capital

- Nigerian and Ghanaian families increasingly transfer land or savings

Black families often pass down:

- debt

- responsibility

- expectation

- emotional pressure

- student loans

- instability

- interrupted assets

- financial trauma

- caregiving obligations

The lifestyles look similar.
The foundations do not.

3. The "First to Do It" Economy

Most Black middle-class adults are:

- the first to graduate

- the first to get a career job

- the first to buy a home

- the first to earn a salary

- the first to stabilize

- the first to escape poverty

- the first to break a cycle

This is incredible.

But it also means:

- no inheritance

- no safety net

- no financial runway

- no fall-back options

- no cushion for mistakes

- no generational capital

- no elder-funded support

- no backup plan if something collapses

Being the first means you are building while carrying.

You are building stability while being the safety net.

This is not the traditional middle-class experience.

---

4. The Silent Burden of Support

Black middle-class life often includes invisible responsibilities:

- helping parents financially

- helping siblings through emergencies

- supporting family during instability

- paying funeral costs

- stepping in during crises

- being the emotional anchor

- navigating family guilt

- being expected to elevate everyone else

This is not because Black families are irresponsible. It is because structural denial created generations of financial fragility.

So the first person to stabilize becomes:

- the provider

- the guide

- the bank

- the rescuer

- the parent to the parents

- the emotional center

No other middle class in America carries this· combination of pressure.

---

5. Homeownership Is Not Equal

Homeownership is the symbol of middle-class life. But homeownership is not the same across racial lines.

Here is the truth:

- Black neighborhoods appreciate slower

- Black homeowners receive lower appraisals

- Black families pay higher loan rates

- Black homes are undervalued even when identical to white homes

- Black buyers receive fewer favorable lending terms

- Black families face higher foreclosure risk

- Black equity grows slower over time

So even when the middle-class symbol is the same, the middle-class outcome is not.

A white family's home becomes generational leverage.
A Black family's home becomes a financial anchor, with limited growth potential.

Same symbol.
Different result.

---

6. The Stability Gap

The real difference between the Black middle class and others is stability.

White middle-class families generally have:

- savings

- equity

- inheritances

- retirement accounts

- low-interest debt

- family support buffers

Black middle-class families often have:

- high student loan burdens

- higher-interest debt

- less savings

- fewer assets

- limited family support

- more people depending on them

- thinner margins

- higher risk exposure

The gap is not visible on paper.
It is felt in the household.

It shows up as:

- stress

- fear of slipping

- financial anxiety

- overwork

- inability to rest

- lack of room for mistakes

This is the hidden cost of being first.

---

7. The Middle Class Was Never the Goal for Other Groups

For Jewish, white, Asian, Middle Eastern, and many African immigrant families, the middle class is not the finish line.

It is the beginning.

They aim for:

- ownership

- equity

- investment

- business control

- compounding

- asset transfer

Black families were told to aim for:

- education

- safe neighborhoods

- good jobs

- college degrees

- respectability

- stability

- survival

We aimed for the symbol.
Others aimed for the foundation.

You were not behind.
You were aiming at different targets because the system positioned the target differently.

---

8. The Truth About Black Middle-Class Progress

Here is the truth the country avoids:

The Black middle class is one of the greatest achievements in American history.

Not because of material goods.
Not because of lifestyle.
But because it was built:

- without inheritance

- without land

- without passed-down wealth

- without early ownership

- without generational guidance

- without institutional support

- without financial protection

- while carrying family responsibilities

- while navigating racial bias

- while challenging structural blockages

What other group built so much with so little?

The Black middle class is proof of capacity, not completion.

You are not behind.
You are the beginning.

---

9. The Path Forward

The Black middle class is not an endpoint.
It is a launch pad.

You are the foundation your family never had.
You are the first wealth builder.
You are the one who breaks the cycle.
You are the one who begins the shift from:

- income to assets

- survival to ownership

- stability to strategy

- respectability to infrastructure

And the next chapters will show you exactly how to turn your middle-class foundation into generational wealth.

Because this is your moment.
Your family's story changes here.
Not with perfection.
With awareness.

Chapter 16: The 100-Year Blueprint

How First-Generation Black Wealth Builders Create What Was Never Built Before

Every group with lasting wealth follows a pattern.

The pattern is not magic.
The pattern is not luck.
The pattern is not a secret.

It is a blueprint.

A simple one.
A repeatable one.
A generational one.

The reason it feels unfamiliar is that Black Americans were denied the chance to practice it for 400 years.
Not because we lacked the skill.
Not because we lacked the intelligence.
Not because we lacked the discipline.

We lacked the runway.

This chapter gives you the runway.

This is how generational wealth is engineered.

---

1. The Goal: Wealth That Outlives You

Most people focus on:

- income goals

- job promotions

- lifestyle upgrades

- year-by-year survival

This is understandable when you are the first.
But generational wealth requires a different lens.

The question is not:

"How much can I earn?"

It is:

"What can I build that my children and
grandchildren can inherit, protect, and multiply?"

Wealth is not how much money you make.
It is how long your decisions last.

---

2. The Formula Every Wealthy Group Uses

Every generationally wealthy family follows the same three-step pattern:

Step 1. Build stability

Savings, insurance, emergency funds, boundaries, clarity, structure.

Step 2. Build ownership

Business equity, investment accounts, real estate, intellectual property, digital assets.

Step 3. Transfer knowledge and systems

Financial literacy, decision frameworks, family documents, lineage expectations, shared vision.

That is the blueprint.

Stability.
Ownership.
Transfer.

Every community that wins follows this arc.

Black families were forced into survival, which delayed the first step.
But today, for the first time, the steps are open again.

3. The 100-Year Lens

Here is what shifts when you think in 100-year terms:

- you stop buying to impress

- you start buying to preserve

- you stop focusing on income

- you start building assets

- you stop racing other people

- you start building your lineage

- you stop fearing slow progress

- you start valuing compounding

- you stop making emotional money decisions

- you start making generational ones

The 100-year lens removes pressure.
It replaces urgency with direction.

Because you are not trying to win the next 5 years. You are trying to transform the next five generations.

---

4. The Four Generational Roles

Every 100-year blueprint includes four generational roles.
You can only play one of them.

Role 1. The Breaker
You break the cycles.
You take the hits.
You fight the battles.
You correct the miseducation.
You build the first foundation.

This is the role you occupy.

Role 2. The Builder
Your children build on your stability.
They expand ownership.
They deepen literacy.
They add structure and assets.

Role 3. The Protector
The next generation protects the wealth.
They preserve the systems.
They manage the assets responsibly.

Role 4. The Multiplier
This generation scales the wealth.
They grow the businesses, investments, and family portfolio.

White families started this cycle centuries ago.
Asian and Jewish families have perfected it.
Black Americans are just now entering it.

You are the first generation to be both Breakers and Builders.

That is the challenge.
That is the honor.

---

5. The First-Generation Advantage

Most people believe first-generation wealth building is a disadvantage.

It is not.

Because:

- you are hungry

- you are aware

- you are intentional

- you are not entitled

- you know struggle

- you know sacrifice

- you know instability

- you know survival

- you know resilience

- you know how to create from nothing

These qualities give first-generation Black builders a level of hunger and precision that children of wealth rarely possess.

Your disadvantage becomes your advantage once you have direction.

---

6. The Four Pillars of a 100-Year Plan

Every generational blueprint is built on four pillars:

Pillar 1. Family Stability

Insurance
Emergency funds
Clear roles
Clear boundaries
Legal documents

Financial communication
Family expectations
Health and wellness
Emotional literacy

A stable family becomes an economic engine.

Pillar 2. Ownership and Assets

Business equity
Investment accounts
Real estate
Digital property
Intellectual property
Savings and reserves
Trusts
Retirement accounts
Stock portfolios

Ownership is the engine of generational wealth.

Pillar 3. Financial Education and Literacy

Teaching children early
Normalizing money talk
Shared family meetings
Understanding debt
Understanding investing
Understanding risk
Understanding taxes
Understanding cash flow

This is the blueprint wealthy families do not skip.

Pillar 4. Institutional Thinking

Family foundations
Scholarships
Investment clubs
Family LLCs
Family banks
Group economics
Ownership collectives

Wealthy families think like institutions.
Not individuals.

This is the shift Black families were denied, until
now.

---

7. The Long View Makes the Short Term Easier

When you think in five-year terms:

- mistakes feel permanent

- setbacks feel personal

- delays feel like failure

- comparison feels unavoidable

- anxiety increases

- progress feels slow

When you think in 100-year terms:

- setbacks mean nothing

- slow progress is still progress

- consistency matters more than speed

- you stop rushing

- you stop comparing

- you start planning

- you start building

A 100-year view gives you patience with yourself and precision with your decisions.

---

8. Your Children Are Your First Investors

Your children will not invest money into your life. They will invest meaning into your legacy.

They absorb:

- how you handle crisis

- how you handle money

- how you handle mistakes

- how you build

- how you recover

- how you plan

- how you move

- how you teach

- how you respond to pressure

Children do not inherit money first.
They inherit patterns.

What you normalize becomes their baseline.
What you teach becomes their instinct.
What you correct becomes their advantage.

They inherit your decisions long before they inherit
your assets.

9. Wealth is a Relay, Not a Race

This is the line that changes everything:

You will not finish the race, but you must run your leg with excellence.

Wealth is not won in one lifetime.
It is built through structured handoffs.

Your job is to:

- clean the starting line

- remove barriers

- create clarity

- pass down knowledge

- pass down assets

- pass down documented systems

- pass down direction

If you do that, you have done what no generation before you was allowed to do.

10. The Blueprint Begins With You

Your ancestors survived without a blueprint.
You build because you finally have one.

You are not behind.
You are the first.
You are the foundation.
You are the turning point.

Your family's wealth story begins with you, but it will not end with you.

This is the 100-year shift.

Chapter 17: The Formula Every Wealthy Group Uses

The Universal Patterns of Generational Success

Wealthy families around the world come from diverse cultures, backgrounds, and histories.

But their **systems** look almost identical.

The languages change.
The rituals change.
The origin stories change.

The formula does not.

This chapter explains the patterns that:

- Jewish families

- Asian families

- Indian families

- White multi-generational families

- Caribbean immigrant families

- African immigrant families

- Middle Eastern families

use to build wealth consistently across generations.

You will see quickly that these are not secrets.
They are structures.

And structures can be learned.

---

1. They Build Around the Family, Not the Individual

Every wealthy group puts the family at the center of its financial decisions.

They focus on:

- family identity

- family roles

- family expectations

- family responsibilities

- family long-term goals

- family stability

This creates:

- shared purpose

- shared accountability

- shared resilience

- shared vision

When the family is the unit, outcomes multiply.

In Black communities, survival often made us focus on individuals instead of family systems.

That shift begins with structure.

---

2. They Talk About Money Early and Often

In wealthy families:

- money is normal conversation

- children learn real numbers

- investing is taught early

- budgets are understood young

- family meetings are routine

- financial decisions are explained

- assets are discussed openly

There is no mystery.
There is no secrecy.
There is no shame.

Black families historically avoided money talk because the topic carried pain, lack, and pressure.

This is where the generational cycle breaks.

---

3. They Prioritize Ownership Over Lifestyle

Every wealthy group practices the same hierarchy:

Assets first.
Lifestyle later.

This means:

- buy the business before the car

- buy real estate before luxury

- invest before vacation upgrades

- build savings before symbols

- acquire assets before status

Ownership creates power.
Lifestyle creates appearance.

Wealthy families choose power.

---

4. They Use Debt Strategically, Not Emotionally

Debt is a tool.

Wealthy groups use debt to:

- acquire assets

- secure leverage

- expand businesses

- build credit intentionally

- preserve liquidity

- minimize taxes

They do not use debt for:

- image

- approval

- comfort

- temporary relief

- emotional spending

- social comparison

This is where many first-generation Black families lose ground, because debt is marketed to us as access, not leverage.

But leverage is learned.

---

5. They Invest Early and Continuously

Every wealthy group practices:

- monthly investing

- long-term holding

- compound interest

- diversified portfolios

- patience with growth

- consistency over perfection

There is no "right moment."
There is only the practice.

Black wealth was delayed by a lack of access and a lack of inherited knowledge.
Now the access exists.
The practice must catch up.

---

6. They Focus on Professions With Leverage

Across cultures, wealthy families choose paths that create:

- high income

- stability

- transferable skills

- professional credibility

- long-term security

Common choices include:

- medicine

- law

- engineering

- finance

- accounting

- technology

- education leadership

- entrepreneurship

This creates:

- reliable income

- respect

- pathways for business

- knowledge that compounds

Oppression pushed Black talent into:

- sports

- entertainment

- service work

- low-wage jobs

- unstable sectors

This was not because of preference, but because of historical restriction.

The blueprint is wide open now.

---

7. They Build Multiple Streams of Income, Not Multiple Jobs

Wealthy families build:

- rental income

- investment income

- business income

- royalties

- intellectual property

- dividends

- licensing

Multiple **streams**, not multiple hours.

Time is limited.
Income streams are not.

Black first-generation builders often create multiple jobs because survival taught us to value effort over leverage.

This mindset shifts completely in this chapter.

---

8. They Use Group Economics

This is crucial.

Wealthy groups collaborate:

- family businesses

- pooled investments

- rotating credit circles

- shared resources

- funded startups

- family loans

- community institutions

- investment clubs

They do not try to win alone.

Black communities were intentionally fragmented. This disrupted our ability to pool capital.

The blueprint brings the collective back.

---

9. They Document Everything

Every wealthy family keeps documents:

- wills

- trusts

- insurance

- financial plans

- tax strategies

- business operating agreements

- family values

- investment policies

- succession plans

Nothing is left to confusion or assumption.

Documentation prevents conflict, protects assets, and ensures the next generation does not start over.

Black families often rely on memory, tradition, or verbal agreements.

Documents change everything.

---

10. They Think in Decades, Not Years

This is the master key.

Wealthy families:

- plan long term

- invest long term

- build businesses long term

- make decisions long term

- structure family roles long term

Decades.
Not years.

Black wealth was forced into short-term thinking because survival demanded immediacy.

But once stability arrives, the mindset must expand.

You are not planning the next two years.
You are building the next two generations.

The Lesson of Chapter 17

There is no mystery.
There is no magic.
There is no secret society.

There are only patterns.

Patterns that were denied to Black families for centuries.
Patterns that wealthy groups repeat with predictable results.
Patterns you can adopt starting today.

This chapter is not about comparison.
It is about clarity.

Wealth is not cultural.
Wealth is structural.

And structure can be learned, taught, practiced, and passed down.

Are We Copying or Reclaiming?

Some people may ask whether adopting these patterns means copying what other groups do.
The answer is simple.
Wealth is not cultural.
Wealth is structural in every community that practices it.

These patterns are universal economic laws that every successful community follows in its own way. Black Americans had our own blueprint, too: Black Wall Street, Durham, Rosewood, and dozens of thriving ecosystems that proved our capacity long before integration.

We are not copying anyone.
We are reclaiming what was denied, restoring what was interrupted, and building our own version with our culture, our values, and our future in mind.

This is not imitation.
This is reconstruction.

Chapter 18: Building Black Ownership in the Modern Economy

The Assets, Opportunities, and Pathways That Finally Level the Playing Field

For most of American history, Black families were denied access to the assets that create generational wealth:

- land

- home equity

- business ownership

- financial markets

- institutional credit

- property appreciation

- investment accounts

- protected inheritance

Ownership was legally, financially, and structurally blocked.

But today, for the first time in 400 years, ownership is accessible in ways our ancestors could not imagine.

Not evenly.
Not perfectly.
Not without obstacles.

But access exists, and the modern economy has opened doors that do not require:

- gatekeepers

- approval

- networks

- pedigree

- inheritance

- perfect credit

- large capital

We are living in the most ownership-friendly moment Black Americans have ever had.

This chapter explains exactly how to use it.

---

1. The Three Types of Ownership That Matter Most Today

There are hundreds of ways to make money.
But only three categories build generational wealth.

A. Business Ownership

This includes:

- service businesses

- online brands

- consulting

- ecommerce

- agencies

- AI-enabled businesses

- content-based businesses

- intellectual property

Business income multiplies faster than salary and is not limited by hours.

B. Asset Ownership

This includes:

- stocks

- index funds

- ETFs

- retirement accounts

- real estate

- syndications

- REITs

- private equity (later on)

These assets grow without you.

C. Digital Ownership

This is the most revolutionary category of the modern era:

- digital products

- courses

- ebooks

- memberships

- community platforms

- newsletters

- digital art

- AI-based tools

- audio programs

- licensing and royalties

Digital ownership is the lowest-barrier path to generational wealth ever created.

Every first-generation builder should be leveraging at least ONE of these categories.

---

2. The End of Gatekeepers and the Rise of Permissionless Wealth

In our parents' and grandparents' time, ownership required:

- bank approval

- industry credentials

- powerful networks

- physical locations

- large capital

- institutional validation

That era is dead.

Today:

- you can launch a digital product in a day

- you can start a business with zero inventory

- you can record a podcast with your phone

- you can publish a book without a publisher

- you can sell knowledge without a degree

- you can invest in index funds with ten dollars

- you can build an audience without connections

- you can learn any skill for free online

This is unprecedented access.

Not equal access, but open access.

Black prosperity no longer depends on institutional permission.

---

3. The New Black Ownership Advantage

Black Americans bring unique strengths into the modern economy:

- creativity

- cultural influence

- storytelling

- community leadership

- resilience

- adaptability

- lived experience

- problem-solving

- authenticity

- innovation

These strengths translate into economic leverage today because:

- authenticity sells

- storytelling builds audience

- lived experience is valuable

- cultural leadership shapes markets

- content creation is currency

- niche expertise is monetizable

For the first time, the marketplace rewards what we naturally do well.

This is the reversal.

---

4. Digital Products: The Fastest Path to Ownership

Digital ownership changes everything.

You can create:

- ebooks

- audio guides

- courses

- templates

- membership groups

- paid newsletters

- coaching programs

- toolkits

- digital art

- AI-generated assets

Benefits:

- no inventory

- no gatekeepers

- low startup cost

- high profit margin

- scalable

- global reach

- compounding value

For Black first-generation builders, this is a wealth shortcut that did not exist before 2010.

Every Black household should have at least one digital product in the next decade.

---

5. Business Ownership: The Old Reliable Pillar

Businesses have always been the backbone of Black economic power, from:

- Tulsa

- Richmond

- Chicago Bronzeville

- Harlem Renaissance businesses

- HBCU ecosystems

- Black churches

- barbershops and salons

- hospitality and service companies

But now, you do not need:

- a storefront

- inventory

- employees

- a big loan

- a lease

Service-based and digital-first businesses are the most accessible forms:

Examples:

- consulting

- content editing

- social media management

- local services

- AI-enhanced services

- marketing agencies

- coaching

- creative production

- real estate locator services

- virtual assistance

Business ownership turns your knowledge into income.

---

6. Real Estate in the Modern Era

Real estate is still a wealth builder, but the playbook has changed.

Black buyers were targeted with predatory lending in the 1990s and 2000s.
Now the safer and more scalable routes are:

- house hacking

- duplex, triplex, and fourplex ownership

- real estate co-ops

- investment clubs

- REITs

- syndications

- fractional ownership

Ownership matters more than "dream home" aesthetics.

The goal is equity, not image.

---

7. Intellectual Property: The New Black Wall Street

Black creativity built:

- music

- fashion

- entertainment

- culture

- aesthetics

- language

- social influence

But much of the profit went to:

- labels

- corporations

- publishers

- platforms

- agencies

Today, intellectual property can be owned directly:

- books

- podcasts

- songs

- scripts

- designs

- characters

- frameworks

- shows

- animations

- branded concepts

This is ownership that can be licensed, franchised, and inherited.

IP is the new Tulsa.
And nobody can burn it down.

---

8. The Blueprint for Black Modern Ownership

Here is the simplest ownership roadmap for first-generation wealth builders:

Year 1: Build skill and stability

Reduce debt, increase literacy, stabilize income.

Year 2: Acquire your first assets

Start investing consistently.

Year 3: Launch a small business or digital product

Create your first ownership vehicle.

Year 4–10: Scale your assets

Grow your investments, expand your business, and build IP.

Year 10-20: Institutionalize

Trusts, family structures, documentation, succession plans.

This is how wealth becomes generational, not accidental.

The Lesson of Chapter 18

Ownership is no longer elite.
Ownership is no longer distant.
Ownership is no longer something Black families discuss only in theory.

Ownership is accessible.
Ownership is strategic.
Ownership is necessary.
Ownership is cultural survival.
Ownership is the foundation of freedom.

And for the first time in American history, Black families can build ownership faster, safer, and smarter than ever before.

Chapter 19: The New Rules of Black Wealth

What Works Now, What No Longer Works, and What You Must Do Differently

For years, Black wealth advice has been based on outdated assumptions:

- work hard

- get a degree

- get a good job

- save money

- buy a home

- retire at 65

This advice was not wrong.
It was incomplete.
And it was built for an economy that no longer exists.

Today's wealth landscape is faster, more volatile, more digital, and more accessible than ever before.
It rewards:

- speed

- skill

- ownership

- creativity

- leverage

It punishes:

- delay

- rigidity

- old playbooks

- overreliance on employment

- emotional money decisions

This chapter outlines the NEW rules.
The ones wealthy families have already adopted.
The ones Black first-generation builders must master.

---

1. Rule One: Skill Beats Degrees

Degrees used to guarantee upward mobility.
Not anymore.

Today:

- skills create income faster

- skills update with the economy

- skills multiply value

- skills can be learned for free

- skills can be monetized directly

- skills reduce risk

- skills increase adaptability

The modern economy pays for:

- problem solving

- communication

- critical thinking

- technology fluency

- creativity

- analysis

- leadership

- digital competence

- strategy

Degrees are still valuable.
But skills build wealth.

This is the first rule.

---

2. Rule Two: Ownership Beats Employment

Employment is stable.
Ownership is scalable.

Two things have changed:

1. **Jobs no longer guarantee security**

2. **The barriers to ownership have collapsed**

Employment is income.
Ownership is freedom.

Black wealth cannot rely on employment alone because:

- salaries cap

- hours limit income

- layoffs are unpredictable

- industries shift

- automation is rising

- the racial wage gap still exists

- wealth requires equity, not effort

Ownership is not optional.
It is the new baseline.

---

3. Rule Three: Assets Beat Savings

You cannot out-save inflation.
You cannot save your way to generational wealth.
You cannot rely on a bank account to grow your future.

Assets grow.
Savings sit.

Assets appreciate.
Savings lose value.

Assets multiply.
Savings stagnate.

Black families historically trusted savings because:

- we were denied investment access

- we were traumatized by financial loss

- we equated cash with safety

- we feared risk

The new rule:

Put cash into assets, not into hiding.

---

4. Rule Four: Speed Beats Perfection

Perfection is a trap.
Speed creates advantage.

The new economy rewards:

- early investors

- early creators

- early business owners

- early skill adopters

- early movers in new platforms

Black builders often wait until:

- we feel ready

- we feel safe

- we feel certain

- we feel prepared

This delay destroys opportunity.

The new rule:

Start early. Adjust later.

---

5. Rule Five: Your Network Is Your Net Worth

This rule is ancient.
But in the modern digital economy, it is amplified.

Your network is not:

- who you know socially

- who follows you online

- who likes your content

Your network is:

- who trusts you

- who refers you

- who collaborates with you

- who invests in you

- who teaches you

- who opens doors

Black families often struggle with networking because:

- we were excluded from key rooms

- we grew up valuing privacy

- we were taught not to ask for help

- we had limited access

- we carried survival pride

The new rule:

Relationships build wealth faster than talent.

---

6. Rule Six: Brand Beats Resume

This is the reversal.

In the old world, your resume mattered.
In the new world, your brand matters.

Brand means:

- your reputation

- your expertise

- your voice

- your consistency

- your perspective

- your digital presence

- your ability to communicate value

People with strong brands:

- get paid more

- attract opportunities

- build trust faster

- grow networks faster

- earn without applying

- pivot easily

- create leverage

Black identity has always influenced culture.
Now it can influence economics.

---

7. Rule Seven: Simplicity Beats Complexity

Complex plans fail.
Simple plans compound.

Wealthy families use simple rules:

- save consistently

- invest automatically

- live below means

- build ownership

- document decisions

- think long-term

- avoid unnecessary debt

Black first-generation builders often feel pressure to:

- do everything at once

- juggle too many goals

- operate without clarity

The new rule:

Simplify.
Stabilize.
Scale.

---

8. Rule Eight: Leverage Beats Labor

Labor pays you once.
Leverage pays you forever.

Leverage includes:

- digital products

- recurring income

- audio/video assets

- intellectual property

- real estate equity

- automation

- outsourcing

- AI tools

- code

- licensing

- content

Leverage is how wealth multiplies without burnout.

Black families have historically been overworked because the system depended on our labor.

This is the shift:

Stop relying on labor.
Start building leverage.

9. Rule Nine: Long-Term Beats Urgent

Urgency is survival energy.
Long-term thinking is wealth energy.

Wealth builders:

- delay gratification

- invest consistently

- protect assets

- plan for family

- avoid emotional spending

- think in decades

This is where Black wealth begins to stabilize.

The new rule:

Play the long game.
Let compounding work.
Let time do the heavy lifting.

10. Rule Ten: Information Beats Imitation

This is the core idea.

Imitating rich lifestyles keeps you broke. Understanding wealthy systems makes you rich.

Information today is free, abundant, and accessible:

- YouTube

- podcasts

- books

- courses

- mentors

- online communities

- free education platforms

- AI tools

Black progress accelerates when we learn:

- how systems work

- how money moves

- how assets grow

- how families build dynasties

The new rule:

Learn the rules.
Then rewrite them for your family.

The Lesson of Chapter 19

The old playbook served a generation that needed stability.
The new playbook serves a generation that needs ownership.

Black wealth is not about repeating what worked in 1970.
It is about mastering what works now.

You are not behind.
You are in the right era.
With the right tools.
And the right access.
At the right moment.

The rules changed in your favor.
And you are ready for this moment.

Chapter 20: The Economic Power of Healing and Identity

Why Wealth Is Impossible Without Emotional Restoration

Most financial books pretend that money is only about numbers.

But for Black first-generation builders, money is also about:

- memory

- trauma

- identity

- family roles

- protection

- fear

- self-worth

- belonging

- survival

- expectation

When trauma goes unaddressed, money becomes emotional.
When identity is unclear, money becomes reactive.
When healing is avoided, wealth becomes unstable.

This chapter explains why emotional restoration is not optional; it is an economic strategy.

Because the moment you heal, your financial decisions change.
Your relationship with money changes.
Your standards change.
Your boundaries change.
Your goals change.
Your patience changes.
Your courage changes.
Your vision changes.

Healing is not soft work.
Healing is infrastructure.

---

1. The Trauma-Wealth Connection

Black Americans inherited trauma that was:

- unspoken

- unprocessed

- unaddressed

- untreated

- unnamed

Generational trauma creates predictable financial behaviors:

- fear of risk

- fear of loss

- fear of asking for help

- fear of trying something new

- overworking

- underearning

- self-sabotage

- guilt around success

- lack of boundaries

- rescuing others at personal expense

- shame around money

- hiding financial struggles

- performing stability

- emotional spending

- avoiding investing

- distrust in institutions

- survival-based decisions

These behaviors are not personality flaws.
They are trauma responses dressed as financial choices.

Healing interrupts the pattern.

---

2. Why Identity Shapes Wealth

Here is a truth most people overlook:

**People do not build wealth from who they pretend to be.
They build wealth from who they believe they are.**

Identity determines:

- what you feel worthy of

- what you pursue

- what you tolerate

- what you avoid

- what you believe you can learn

- what opportunities you chase

- what risks you take

- how you handle money

- how you handle pressure

- how you handle failure

If your identity was shaped by survival, you will:

- think small

- avoid exposure

- fear failure

- minimize yourself

- undercharge

- overgive

- ignore rest

- self-impose limits

- settle for stability over abundance

Healing reshapes identity.
Identity reshapes behavior.
Behavior reshapes wealth.

---

3. The First-Generation Emotional Load

First-generation Black wealth builders carry emotional weight that other groups do not:

- the pressure to succeed for the whole family

- the fear of slipping back into poverty

- the guilt of surpassing loved ones

- the responsibility of being the financial anchor

- the expectation to fix everything

- the burden of being the example

- the stress of being the first to navigate new spaces

- the lack of emotional support

- the isolation of being the only one

- the need to perform strength

- the fear of asking for help

These emotional realities directly influence:

- spending

- saving

- investing

- business decisions

- career moves

- boundaries

- stress levels

- long-term planning

You cannot build generational wealth while carrying invisible emotional debt.

4. Healing Creates Financial Clarity

When you heal:

- you stop making emotional financial decisions

- you stop performing success

- you stop rescuing everyone

- you stop tolerating instability

- you stop attaching your worth to your lifestyle

- you stop associating rest with weakness

Healing creates clarity.

Clarity creates structure.

Structure creates wealth.

5. The Role of Therapy, Faith, and Community

Healing for Black families often requires a blend of three forces:

A. Therapy

For:

- trauma

- anxiety

- fear

- money wounds

- emotional habits

- identity confusion

Therapy helps you see patterns you inherited but never chose.

B. Faith

For:

- hope

- grounding

- self-worth

- safety

- identity

- community

- meaning

Faith strengthens you in places logic cannot reach.

C. Community

For:

- accountability

- connection

- cultural resilience

- shared experience

- emotional support

- practical advice

Black wealth is too heavy to build alone.

You need a circle.

---

6. Healing Rewrites Your Money Story

Every person has a money story.

Some stories sound like:

- "I cannot risk losing anything."

- "I have to help everyone."

- "I cannot let people see me struggle."

- "I will never have enough."

- "I am behind."

- "I cannot fail."

- "I cannot depend on anyone."

Healing rewrites the internal script to:

- "I can build safely."

- "I deserve abundance."

- "I am allowed to learn."

- "I am allowed to rest."

- "I can receive help."

- "I can invest without fear."

- "I do not have to save everyone."

- "My future can look different."

Wealth is not only built from external opportunity. It is built from internal permission.

---

7. Healing Strengthens All Four Generational Roles

From Chapter 16, healing strengthens:

The Breaker (you)
You stop repeating trauma-based financial patterns.

The Builder
You create wealth with clarity instead of pressure.

The Protector
You operate with judgment instead of fear.

The Multiplier
You make bold moves from stability, not insecurity.

Healing strengthens the lineage.

---

8. Identity as Economic Power

Black identity has always been:

- creative

- resilient

- adaptive

- innovative

- expressive

- powerful

But miseducation distorted identity into:

- self-doubt

- self-minimization

- impostor syndrome

- fear of ambition

- survival thinking

- cultural fragmentation

Economic power requires identity restoration.

Because when you know who you are:

- you negotiate differently

- you invest differently

- you price differently

- you speak differently

- you lead differently

- you plan differently

- you dream differently

- you build differently

- you recover differently

Identity fuels elevation.

The Lesson of Chapter 20

You cannot build generational wealth on emotional instability.
You cannot scale while you are fractured.
You cannot plan clearly when you are carrying unprocessed pain.

Healing is not a detour.
Healing is not a luxury.
Healing is not separate from wealth.

Healing is an economic strategy.

Because when the trauma quiets, the vision sharpens.

When the identity strengthens, the wealth accelerates.

You are not behind.
You are healing into the person your lineage needed.
And the wealth follows that transformation.

Chapter 21: Building the Black Family Institution

How to Turn Your Household Into a Wealth Engine

Every wealthy group treats the family like an institution, not a collection of individuals.

An institution has:

- structure

- roles

- rules

- documentation

- meetings

- goals

- processes

- values

- communication

- succession

- accountability

Most Black families were denied this because our lineage was disrupted repeatedly:

- slavery

- forced migration

- Jim Crow

- redlining

- mass incarceration

- economic instability

- survival-based parenting

- family fragmentation

We were taught to survive as individuals, not to operate as institutions.

But wealth is built by institutions.

This chapter shows exactly how to build one.

---

1. The Family Is the First Economic System

Before banks.
Before businesses.
Before investments.

The family is the first:

- school

- training ground

- safety net

- support system

- economic incubator

- emotional foundation

- wealth starter

- wealth protector

When the family is stable, wealth grows.
When the family is fragile, wealth leaks.

Turning your family into an institution begins with this truth:

The family must be the primary unit, not the individual.

---

2. The Eight Pillars of a Family Institution

A true family institution is built on eight pillars:

Pillar One: Vision

Where the family is going and why.
A shared future that guides decisions.

Pillar Two: Values

What the family stands for and refuses to compromise on.
Values dictate behavior.

Pillar Three: Roles

Clear assignments so no one carries everything, and no one carries nothing.
Roles minimize chaos.

Pillar Four: Communication

Regular, honest conversations about money, goals, and responsibilities.
Communication stabilizes the system.

Pillar Five: Documentation

Wills, trusts, insurance, budgets, written plans, and family records.
Documentation protects the institution.

Pillar Six: Financial Literacy

Teaching children the rules of money early and consistently.
Literacy multiplies stability.

Pillar Seven: Systems

Processes for saving, investing, budgeting, discipline, family meetings, and decision-making.
Systems prevent emotional or reactive choices.

Pillar Eight: Accountability

Everyone is contributing to the health of the household, not consuming from it.
Accountability preserves structure.

These eight pillars prepare your family to build wealth that survives beyond you.

---

3. The Family Vision Statement

Every wealthy family has a defined vision that directs how the family moves.

It answers:

- Who are we

- What do we value

- What are we building

- What do we want for future generations

A Black family institution might say:

- We build stability

- We invest in knowledge

- We prioritize ownership

- We protect each other

- We pass down assets and wisdom

- We create opportunities

This vision anchors everything.
It lifts the family from survival to strategy.

---

4. The Family Roles Framework

Roles are how you eliminate chaos.

Black families often collapse because:

- one person carries everything

- roles shift based on crisis

- boundaries are unclear

- children parent parents

- emotional labor is uneven

- financial expectations are unspoken

In a family institution, roles are defined:

The Stabilizer

Handles household operations.
Ensures bills, documents, and systems run smoothly.

The Educator

Teaches literacy, values, identity, and responsibility.

The Builder

Grows income, assets, and business opportunities.

The Protector

Manages insurance, security, safety, and planning.

The Communicator

Leads family meetings, conflict resolution, and transparency.

These roles can shift, but they cannot disappear.

When roles are clear, families grow.
When roles are unclear, families collapse.

---

5. The Family Meeting Ritual

Every wealthy family across cultures holds regular meetings.

They discuss:

- money

- goals

- plans

- responsibilities

- progress

- upcoming decisions

- family health

The meeting is not a lecture.
It is a ritual.

For Black families, this ritual replaces silence with structure.

Meeting agenda example:

1. Quick check-in

2. Review of goals

3. Review of finances

4. Review of upcoming decisions

5. Questions, feedback, clarity

6. Share something learned

7. Plan for the next meeting

Consistency creates culture.

---

6. Documentation: The Family's Armor

Black families lose more wealth from lack of documentation than from lack of income.

Documentation protects:

- wealth

- clarity

- legacy

- property

- assets

- decisions

- children

- business

A family institution must have:

- a will

- a trust

- life insurance

- beneficiaries updated

- power of attorney

- medical directives

- written financial plan

- digital passwords accessible

- succession plans

- family values statement

Documentation is not a luxury.
It is protection.

---

7. The Money Culture Inside the Home

Your family must know:

- money is normal to discuss

- wealth is expected

- literacy is required

- transparency is standard

- budgeting is collective

- investing is routine

- saving is not punishment

- ownership is a priority

- generosity is structured, not pressured

Black homes often avoided money talk because it triggered:

- pain

- shame

- conflict

- fear

- comparison

- scarcity

In an institution, money is neutral.

It is a tool.
Not a secret.
Not a weapon.

Not a burden.
Not a symbol of power.

Just a tool for building.

---

8. Preparing Children for Wealth

Children in wealthy families are not left to guess.
They are prepared.

They learn:

- how money works

- how assets grow

- how taxes function

- how business operates

- how investing compounds

- how to lead

- how to communicate

- how to handle pressure

- how to fail and rebuild

- how to think long-term

Black children rarely receive this because parents were in survival mode.

Now you get to change that.

---

9. Family Institutions Survive What Individuals Cannot

This chapter exists because:

- jobs collapse

- industries shift

- health changes

- markets fluctuate

- family members age

- emergencies occur

- wealth cycles break

- trauma reappears

An institution absorbs the shock.
A disorganized household does not.

Institution means stability.
Household means volatility.

You are building stability.

The Lesson of Chapter 21

Black families were denied the structure required to build generational wealth.
Now you are building it.

You are not behind.
You are institutionalizing your bloodline.
You are creating clarity where there was confusion.
You are creating structure where there was survival.
You are creating order where there was improvisation.
You are creating legacy where there was loss.

Your family becomes the institution your ancestors never got to build.

Chapter 22: The Money Conversations Black Families Must Have

How Communication Becomes the Foundation of Wealth

Black families historically avoided money conversations because money was tied to:

- shame

- fear

- trauma

- arguments

- instability

- scarcity

- secrecy

- unpredictability

Silence became the norm.
Avoidance became protection.
Survival became the language.

But generational wealth cannot grow in silence.

Money conversations are the **infrastructure** of a family institution.
They turn confusion into clarity.
They turn pressure into teamwork.
They turn individual struggles into collective solutions.

This chapter equips you with the exact conversations Black families must have.

Not someday.
Now.

---

1. The Five Reasons Black Families Avoid Money Talks

Understanding the silence is the first step.

A. Money was a source of trauma

Bills. Shutoff notices. Evictions. Layoffs. Debt. Money was unpredictable and painful.

B. Parents tried to protect children from stress

Silence felt safer than truth.

C. Talking about money was seen as rude or disrespectful

Cultural politeness replaced generational literacy.

D. Survival left no space for planning

When every month is uncertain, long-term conversations feel impossible.

E. Past generations had no blueprint to pass down

You cannot teach what you never learned.

These reasons are not failures.
They are the result of history.

Now we build something better.

---

2. The Six Conversations Every Black Family Needs to Have

These conversations turn a household into a functioning economic system.

They are simple, repeatable, and high-impact.
They change everything.

Conversation One: Where We Are Now

This is the starting point.

Every family must know:

- what we earn

- what we spend

- what we owe

- what we own

- what we prioritize

This conversation removes fear.
Silence creates anxiety.
Clarity creates stability.

Conversation Two: What We Value

Most financial conflicts do not stem from money.
It comes from mismatched values.

Values answer questions like:

- Do we value ownership

- Do we value freedom

- Do we value education

- Do we value stability

- Do we value experiences

- Do we value service

- Do we value discipline

- Do we value generational planning

Values determine direction.
Direction determines decisions.
Decisions determine wealth.

Conversation Three: The Cost of Our Goals

Black families often have dreams without numbers attached.

The question is simple:

- How much do our goals cost

- How long will it take

- What systems must support it

- What sacrifices are required

- What income must grow

- What debt must shrink

Turning dreams into numbers turns hope into plans.

Conversation Four: The Legacy Plan

The most challenging, most avoided conversation is about:

- wills

- insurance

- trusts

- property

- guardianship

- end-of-life decisions

Many Black families lose everything because no one planned.

This conversation prevents:

- chaos

- conflict

- confusion

- forced sales

- court battles

- financial collapse

Legacy is not the end.
Legacy is the beginning of stability for the next generation.

Conversation Five: Money and Identity

Money shapes identity.
Identity shapes money.

Families must talk about:

- what success looks like

- what stability feels like

- what money meant growing up

- what fears are attached to money

- what wounds influence decisions

- what beliefs hold us back

These conversations heal the emotional blocks around wealth.

Conversation Six: How We Handle Emergencies

Emergencies reveal the strength of the family institution.

Every family must decide:

- where the emergency fund lives

- what counts as an emergency

- who has access

- what happens if someone loses a job

- what happens if someone gets sick

- how the family will support each other

- how the family will protect children

Planning reduces panic.
Panic destroys wealth.

---

3. The Communication Rules That Create Wealth

Talking about money is not enough.
You need rules.

Here are the rules that keep communication healthy:

A. No blame

Blame shuts down conversation.

B. No shame

Shame kills transparency.

C. No secrecy

Secrets destroy wealth.

D. No silence when something is wrong

Early conversations prevent big problems.

E. No emotional punishments

Money talks must be safe spaces.

F. Everyone participates

Wealth is a team sport.

These rules create trust, and trust creates wealth.

---

4. The Money Conversations for Children

Children need language for money early.

Your job is not to pressure them.
Your job is to prepare them.

Teach them:

- saving

- investing

- taxes

- assets

- risk

- planning

- generosity

- work ethic

- budgeting

- responsibility

Children raised with money literacy enter adulthood with confidence instead of fear.

They do not have to repeat your mistakes.
That is the purpose of generational evolution.

---

5. Money Meetings: The Monthly Ritual

This is where it all comes together.

Once a month, the family talks.

Agenda:

1. Review income

2. Review spending

3. Review goals

4. Review challenges

5. Review opportunities

6. Share something learned

7. Plan the next steps

Meetings turn knowledge into action.
Action turns families into institutions.

The Lesson of Chapter 22

Black families did not talk about money because silence felt safe.
Now silence is the danger.

You cannot build wealth with unspoken fears.
You cannot build stability with unasked questions.
You cannot build legacy with hidden decisions.

The family institution thrives where communication flows freely.

You are not behind.
You are teaching your family the conversations that should have existed generations ago.

Chapter 23: The Emotional Rules of Black Wealth Building

How to Protect Your Mind While You Build Your Future

Wealth is not only built with money.
It is also built with emotional strength.

For Black first-generation wealth builders, the emotional demands are higher because the pressures are greater, the expectations are broader, and the identity shifts are more profound.

This chapter explains the emotional rules that protect your peace, growth, and clarity as you build something your family has never seen before.

These rules are not soft.
They are strategic.

---

1. Rule One: Never Tie Your Worth to Your Wealth

If money determines your worth, you will:

- chase validation

- hide your struggles

- fear risk

- panic during setbacks

- overspend to feel confident

- shrink when money is low

- attach identity to income

Black builders were conditioned to believe:

- status equals value

- performance equals identity

- stability equals worth

- income equals manhood

- money equals respect

This mindset collapses under pressure.

Your worth is fixed.
Your money is variable.

When you separate the two, you can build without fear.

2. Rule Two: Do Not Carry Everyone's Burdens

Black first-gen builders often become:

- the family bank

- the family therapist

- the family emergency plan

- the family fixer

- the family hope

- the family symbol of success

This emotional load destroys wealth because:

- you deplete yourself

- you lose focus

- you sacrifice your goals

- you bail out adults repeatedly

- you substitute love for rescue

- you carry guilt for outgrowing people

The rule is simple:

Help strategically, not emotionally.
Support responsibly, not endlessly.

Saving yourself is the foundation of saving your family.

---

3. Rule Three: Failure Is Data, Not Identity

Black children are often raised with:

- perfection pressure

- fear of judgment

- fear of making mistakes

- fear of embarrassment

- consequences for trial and error

So failure becomes:

- shame

- proof of inadequacy

- something to hide

- something to avoid

- something that halts progress

But in wealth building, failure is not a verdict. Failure is information.

It tells you:

- what to adjust

- what to avoid

- what to double down on

- what to refine

Failure is the tuition you pay for generational wisdom.

---

4. Rule Four: Do Not Allow Fear to Become a Financial Strategy

Fear-based decisions look like:

- avoiding investing

- avoiding opportunities

- avoiding leadership

- avoiding risk

- avoiding visibility

- over-saving out of panic

- undercharging because of insecurity

- staying in jobs that limit you

- staying silent to avoid pressure

Fear feels safe, but it is expensive.
It delays wealth.
It sabotages momentum.
It creates financial paralysis.

The rule:

Courage creates compounding.

5. Rule Five: Rest Is a Strategy, Not a Reward

Black families have been conditioned to believe:

- rest is laziness

- rest is a luxury

- rest is unproductive

- rest is earned, not needed

This causes:

- burnout

- irritability

- poor decisions

- emotional instability

- decreased creativity

- mental fatigue

Wealth requires clarity.
Clarity requires rest.

The rule:

If you cannot rest, you cannot rise.

---

6. Rule Six: Protect Your Peace From People Who Live in Chaos

Black first-gen builders often feel obligated to:

- engage in every crisis

- answer every call

- absorb every complaint

- mediate every conflict

- fix generational dysfunction

- stay tied to people who drain them

But peace is fuel.
Chaos is a leak.

Your future depends on boundaries.

Boundaries are not rejection.
Boundaries are respect.
Boundaries protect your potential.
Boundaries preserve your capacity.

The rule:

Distance is sometimes the most loving choice.

---

7. Rule Seven: Do Not Rush What Needs Time

Wealth is slow at first.
Black builders who grew up in survival mode often expect:

- quick wins

- rapid relief

- overnight success

- immediate payoff

When it does not happen, they panic or quit.

But wealth grows in stages:

- stabilization

- discipline

- structure

- investment

- leverage

- compounding

- expansion

You cannot rush seeds.
You can only plant, water, and protect them.

The rule:

Patience is a wealth skill.

---

8. Rule Eight: Celebrate Quietly, Not Performatively

Over-celebration traps Black builders because:

- people expect more from you

- you attract unnecessary pressure

- you invite envy

- you activate guilt

- you feel obligated to help more

- your wins trigger family wounds

- you are judged before you stabilize

Quiet celebration protects your momentum.
It protects your mental health.
It protects your boundaries.
It protects your vision.

The rule:

Celebrate silently until your foundation is unshakeable.

---

9. Rule Nine: Prepare for Emotional Shifts as You Level Up

Building wealth changes:

- how you see yourself

- how your family sees you

- how your friends treat you

- who you relate to

- who you lose

- who you attract

- who you outgrow

These shifts are emotional.
Many Black builders are unprepared for:

- the loneliness

- the guilt

- the misunderstanding

- the separation

- the identity expansion

These feelings are normal.
They are not signs to stop.
They are signs you are evolving.

---

10. Rule Ten: Protect the Future From the Past

Your past created survival habits.
Your future requires strategic habits.

Your past taught you:

- fear

- caution

- silence

- instant gratification

- self-sacrifice

- emotional money habits

Your future demands:

- clarity

- consistency

- structure

- literacy

- boundaries

- long-term thinking

Wealth requires choosing the future version of you over the former version of you.

The rule:

Do not let old patterns lead your new life.

The Lesson of Chapter 23

Wealth is not only a financial journey.
It is an emotional evolution.

You are learning the emotional rules that wealthy
families internalized generations ago.

You are not behind.
You are mastering skills your lineage was never
allowed to learn.
You are building wealth with clarity, not fear.
You are making decisions based on identity rather
than insecurity.
You are protecting your energy, your vision, and
your purpose.

The emotional work is the wealth work.

Chapter 24: How Black Families Break the Cycle for Good

Turning Progress Into Permanence

Breaking the cycle is not only about making more money.
It is about building a system that prevents the next generation from sliding backward.

Black families have often risen, only to collapse again because the structure was fragile.

The cycle breaks when:

- information is shared

- systems are documented

- roles are defined

- assets are protected

- habits are passed down

- emotional wounds are healed

- literacy becomes culture

- identity becomes strength

- opportunities are intentional

Cycle-breaking is not an accident.
It is design.

---

1. The Cycle Breaks When the Knowledge Is Shared

The quickest way for a family to lose wealth:

One person learns everything.
No one else learns anything.

The cycle breaks when knowledge becomes:

- open

- normal

- consistent

- teachable

- repeated

- expected

Every generation must learn:

- how money works

- how assets grow

- how taxes reduce wealth

- how credit supports leverage

- how investing compounds

- how insurance protects

- how real estate multiplies

- how business operates

- how to manage emotions

- how to avoid debt traps

When knowledge is passed down, wealth no longer resets at zero.

---

2. The Cycle Breaks When the Blueprint Is Written Down

Black families lose more wealth from a *lack of documentation* than from any other reason.

To break the cycle permanently, the family must have:

- a written plan

- a written budget

- a written strategy

- a written vision

- a written legacy plan

- a written trust or will

- written instructions for children

- written values

If it is not written:

- it gets forgotten

- it gets misunderstood

- it gets ignored

- it gets lost

- it dies with you

Writing converts ideas into infrastructure.

---

3. The Cycle Breaks When the Family Structure Is Stabilized

A family institution protects wealth by stabilizing:

- communication

- roles

- expectations

- responsibilities

- decision-making

The cycle breaks when every family member knows:

- what they contribute

- what they protect

- what they follow

- what they uphold

Chaos destroys wealth.
Structure protects it.

Stability is strategy.

---

4. The Cycle Breaks When Children Are Prepared, Not Spoiled

Children who inherit money without literacy lose it. Children who inherit literacy without money multiply it.

You break the cycle by preparing children early:

- give them chores

- give them responsibility

- teach them ownership

- teach them saving and investing

- teach them how business works

- teach them how to think for themselves

- teach them not to fear failure

- teach them how to manage money

- teach them how to lead

- teach them how to communicate

A prepared child becomes a protector of the family's future.
An unprepared child becomes the cycle's restart.

---

5. The Cycle Breaks When the Family Stops Romanticizing Struggle

Black families have normalized:

- exhaustion

- overwork

- burnout

- silently suffering

- doing everything alone

- surviving instead of planning

Struggle was necessary in the past.
It is not the blueprint for the future.

You break the cycle by ending the belief that:

- pain is noble

- rest is weakness

- help is dependency

- boundaries are disrespect

- therapy is unnecessary

- wealth is suspicious

When struggle is no longer glorified, stability becomes expected.

---

6. The Cycle Breaks When the Family Learns How to Handle Success

Success can be dangerous without emotional maturity.

Black families often collapse when success arrives because:

- guilt surfaces

- comparison intensifies

- family pressure increases

- self-sabotage activates

- fear rises

- identity shifts cause conflict

- relationships change

Breaking the cycle requires teaching the family:

- how to normalize abundance

- how to maintain boundaries

- how to avoid lifestyle inflation

- how to invest instead of perform

- how to manage attention

- how to stay grounded

- how to grow without guilt

Success becomes sustainable when it is understood.

---

7. The Cycle Breaks When the Family Has Protection Systems

Black families lose wealth because they lack:

- legal protection

- asset protection

- income protection

- emergency funds

- medical directives

- insurance

Protection prevents a setback from becoming a collapse.

Breaking the cycle means putting safety nets in place so that:

- one emergency does not destroy progress

- one illness does not empty savings

- one death does not scatter assets

- one crisis does not reset the next generation

Protection is not fear.
Protection is freedom.

---

8. The Cycle Breaks When the Family Thinks Long-Term

Black first-gen builders often think in survival time:

- days

- weeks

- months

Wealthy families think in legacy time:

- decades

- generations

- 100-year plans

The cycle breaks when families start asking:

- What do we want our last name to mean

- What will our family own 20 years from now

- What problems will our grandchildren never have

- What will we pass down besides money

- How do we prepare our children to lead

Generational thinking creates generational direction.

---

9. The Cycle Breaks When the Family Becomes Intentional About Opportunity

Opportunity is not random.
It is built.

Black families can break the cycle permanently by creating:

- career pipelines

- mentorship systems

- business apprenticeships

- investment clubs

- family-owned properties

- shared financial education

- generational savings plans

- scholarships for family members

- business funding systems

- family networking channels

Opportunity is the opposite of luck.

---

10. The Cycle Breaks When One Person Starts, and Everyone Learns

Cycle-breaking does not require a perfect family. It requires one builder who:

- learns

- leads

- documents

- teaches

- protects

- structures

- communicates

- stabilizes

One person can pull the family forward.
One person can change the direction.
One person can break the pattern.

You are that person.

The Lesson of Chapter 24

Black families have never lacked potential.
We have lacked structure.

The cycle does not break because you make money.
The cycle breaks because you create a system that
makes sure no one ever has to start from zero again.

You are not behind.
You are building what your lineage was never given.
You are creating the clarity your family never had.
You are building the systems your ancestors
dreamed of.
You are transforming the future of your last name.

The cycle ends with you.
The dynasty begins with you.

Chapter 25: The Black Wealth Playbook for the Next 100 Years

A Long-Term Strategy for Generational Stability, Freedom, and Power

The next century will either widen the racial wealth gap or reverse it.
The difference will not be luck, policy, or politics.
It will be design.

The 100-year playbook gives Black families a strategy that outlasts:

- recessions

- market crashes

- inflation cycles

- job layoffs

- gentrification

- political swings

- technological shifts

- systemic resistance

This is not about getting richer.
This is about building a foundation that cannot be broken again.

---

1. The 100-Year Mindset

Wealthy families do not think in:

- months

- years

- job cycles

They think in:

- lineage

- legacy

- decades

- dynasties

Black wealth collapses when each generation starts from zero.

A 100-year plan ensures:

- progress compounds

- mistakes do not reset the family

- knowledge grows

- leadership evolves

- identity strengthens

- assets remain protected

The first rule of the next century is simple:

Stop planning for yourself.
Start planning for your lineage.

---

2. The Six Foundations of a 100-Year Plan

A century-long strategy requires six core foundations:

Foundation One: Identity

A family needs a story, a vision, and values that unify its decisions.

Foundation Two: Literacy

Financial education must be routine, expected, and internalized.

Foundation Three: Stability

No generational plan survives instability.
Stability must be engineered at home.

Foundation Four: Ownership

Assets must transfer from one generation to the next without interruption.

Foundation Five: Documentation

Wills, trusts, passwords, property records, business instructions.
Everything protected. Everything clear.

Foundation Six: Systems

Processes that run even when people falter.
Systems create continuity.

These foundations make the family antifragile.

---

3. The 100-Year Wealth Vehicles

These are the five vehicles that compound over a century.

Vehicle One: Real Estate

Real estate stabilizes the family and anchors future generations.
Land and property are the foundation of endurance.

Vehicle Two: Business Ownership

A family business, even a small one, creates:

- employment

- skills

- tax advantages

- financial literacy

- leadership development

- income streams

A business is a wealth school.

Vehicle Three: Investment Accounts

Compounding turns small amounts into generational assets.
Time matters more than money.

Vehicle Four: Insurance and Protection

Protection ensures one emergency does not destroy the family's momentum.

Vehicle Five: Intellectual Property

Books, courses, music, content, brand assets.
This is the new Black Wall Street.
Digital ownership scales without limit.

---

4. The Family Leadership Model

Every century-long plan needs leaders in each era.

Generation One: The Breaker

Breaks the cycle of survival.

Generation Two: The Builder

Builds stability and wealth systems.

Generation Three: The Protector

Puts legal and financial protections in place.

Generation Four: The Multiplier

Takes the foundation and expands it.

This model prevents regressions.
It prevents collapse.
It keeps the family moving forward.

---

5. The Four Laws of Intergenerational Stability

These laws keep the next century aligned.

Law One: Each Generation Must Leave Instruction

No guesswork.
No confusion.
No silence.

Law Two: Each Generation Must Train Its Children Early

Financial literacy must begin before middle school.

Law Three: Each Generation Must Protect What It Builds

Insurance, trusts, and legal structures cannot be optional.

Law Four: Each Generation Must Reinvent the Strategy

The world changes every decade.
The family must adapt.

These laws prevent stagnation and create resilience.

---

6. The 100-Year Family Infrastructure Plan

Your family should build three infrastructures:

A. Economic Infrastructure

Savings.
Investments.
Property.
Protection.
Income systems.

B. Educational Infrastructure

Literacy systems.
Skill-building.
Work ethic.
Emotional intelligence.
Identity formation.

C. Cultural Infrastructure

Values.
Traditions.
Rituals.
Stories.
Family meetings.
Shared purpose.

An infrastructure survives what individuals cannot.

---

7. The Role of Technology and AI in Black Wealth

AI is the single greatest opportunity for Black wealth in modern history.

It lowers:

- barriers to entry

- cost of business

- cost of creation

- cost of learning

- cost of labor

It increases:

- earning potential

- skill development

- access to opportunity

- scalability

- speed

The next century of Black wealth will be built by people who master:

- digital tools

- automation

- content creation

- data literacy

- online business models

- AI-assisted decision making

AI is not a threat when you use it.
It is a threat when you ignore it.

---

8. The Family Document Set

Every Black family needs a protected family document vault that includes:

- a trust or will

- business instructions

- property documents

- insurance policies

- bank and investment accounts

- passwords

- educational plans

- medical directives

- a family mission statement

- a succession plan

- contact list for advisors

This is the blueprint that prevents chaos.

---

9. The 100-Year Rituals

Because systems are only as strong as the consistency behind them.

Your family should practice:

Annual Wealth Meeting

Full review of assets, goals, and stability.

Quarterly Financial Check-In

Adjust strategy based on the economy and family needs.

Monthly Money Meeting

Household-level planning.

Yearly Literacy Week

Teaching children new skills and principles.

Rituals create stability.
Stability creates momentum.

---

10. The Final Rule: The Family Must Move as One

The next century of Black wealth will be won by families who move like:

- teams

- institutions

- units

- ecosystems

Not random individuals.

When the family moves together:

- knowledge multiplies

- assets protect each other

- stability compounds

- children grow with confidence

- opportunity becomes normal

- legacy becomes inevitable

This is how the next century belongs to us.

The Lesson of Chapter 25

The Black wealth story does not end with you.
It begins with you.

You are not behind.
You are the first generation with the information, access, technology, and strategy to build a 100-year legacy.

Your lineage is shifting because you decided to build what they were never given.

This is the blueprint your ancestors never received.
This is the blueprint your grandchildren will thank you for.
This is the blueprint that finally ends the cycle.

Chapter 26: The Black Wealth Manifesto

A Declaration for the Next Hundred Years

We are the generation that refuses to inherit silence.

We are the generation that refuses to inherit fear.

We are the generation that refuses to inherit the illusions, the limits, the miseducation, and the cycles designed to keep us from knowing our power.

We are the first in our families to see the full truth.
We are the first to understand the story behind the struggle.
We are the first to hold the information, the access, the tools, and the clarity that our ancestors prayed for but were never given.

We do not apologize for being the beginning.
We do not apologize for being the correction.
We do not apologize for being the turning point.

We stand in the legacy of Black builders who created wealth from nothing.
We stand in the legacy of Black families who held together what systems tried to tear apart.
We stand in the legacy of Black minds who dreamed of futures they would not live to see.

And now it is our turn.

THE DECLARATION

We declare that we are not behind.
We declare that we were delayed by design.
We declare that we will not pass that delay to the
next generation.
We declare that wealth is not a miracle.
It is a structure.
It is a discipline.
It is a culture.
It is a decision.

We declare that struggle will no longer define us.
We declare that clarity will replace confusion.
We declare that healing will replace silence.
We declare that structure will replace chaos.
We declare that ownership will replace survival.
We declare that literacy will replace guesswork.

We declare that we will protect our emotional
health, because our minds are assets.
We declare that we will protect our families because
our bloodline is sacred.
We declare that we will protect our children,
because they are the future we are building for.

We declare that we will think in decades.
We will plan in generations.
We will move in unity.
We will build with intention.

We will not shrink.
We will not apologize.
We will not hide.
We will not beg for seats at tables built on our labor.

We build our own.

THE MANIFESTO

1. We build wealth on truth, not illusion.

We refuse to compare ourselves to timelines built on inherited advantage.
We measure ourselves by the cycles we break, the systems we create, and the futures we secure.

2. We treat the family as an institution.

Our households will not be random.
Our decisions will not be isolated.
Our planning will not be unstable.
We operate with roles, order, documentation, and clarity.

3. We embrace ownership as the foundation of freedom.

We own our labor, our time, our skills, our platforms, our content, our property, and our decisions.
Ownership is our baseline, not our aspiration.

4. We master the emotional work.

We release guilt, shame, inherited fear, survival pressure, and identity wounds.
We build with clarity, self-worth, patience, confidence, and wisdom.
The emotional work is the wealth work.

5. We prepare our children early.

We teach them the rules, the risks, the opportunities, the mindset, the discipline, the history, and the vision.
Our children will not guess their way through life.
They will walk in knowledge.

6. We design wealth, not chase it.

Our strategy is long-term.
Our moves are intentional.
Our progress is inevitable.
We do not rush.
We do not panic.
We do not get distracted.
We build slowly, consistently, and permanently.

7. We protect what we build.

We use insurance, trusts, legal structures, documentation, planning, and boundaries.
Wealth without protection is charity, and wealth with protection is legacy.

8. We expand without guilt.

We do not shrink to make others comfortable.
We do not apologize for growth.
We do not dim our ambition.
Success is not betrayal.
Success is responsibility.

9. We move as a community, not as isolated individuals.

We lift.
We teach.
We circulate.
We collaborate.
We share knowledge.
We support progress.
Our unity is our multiplier.

10. We build for the next 100 years.

Our decisions outlive us.
Our actions compound.
Our family name gains weight.
Our lineage gains power.
Our blueprint becomes tradition.

We build with the future in mind and the past in our hands.

WHY THIS BOOK WAS WRITTEN

This manifesto exists because our people have gone too long without what we needed:

A playbook.
A strategy.
A language.
A structure.
A truth.
A correction.
A foundation.

This book was written because Black families have carried questions for generations without receiving answers.

It was written because we were tired of watching our people get blamed for outcomes shaped by history, policy, miseducation, and denial.

It was written because our story needed to be told from the inside, not explained from the outside.

It was written because too many of us spent years searching for the blueprint and found only fragments, not clarity.

It was written because we are the first generation with access, awareness, and opportunity to build what those before us were denied.

It was written to bridge the gap between what our ancestors dreamed of and what our descendants deserve.

This is why this book exists.
To serve.
To clarify.
To empower.
To awaken.
To build.

THE FINAL WORD

We are not behind.
We never were.

We were interrupted.
We were miseducated.
We were delayed.

Now we are informed.
We are intentional.
We are equipped.
We are unified.
We are building.

And nothing can stop a people who finally understand the game, the strategy, the system, the psychology, the history, and the power they have always possessed.

This is the manifesto.
This is the blueprint.
This is the declaration.
This is the shift.

The next century belongs to us.

EPILOGUE

The Return to Ourselves

There is a moment in every generation when the truth becomes impossible to ignore.

A moment when the weight of silence becomes heavier than the discomfort of honesty.
A moment when the patterns of the past no longer feel like the future.
A moment when a people collectively decide that survival is not enough.

This book is the result of that moment.

We have spent centuries carrying stories that did not belong to us, narratives that worked against us, and expectations that limited us.
We inherited the aftershocks of systems we did not create, yet we were expected to thrive without understanding the full history that shaped our starting point.

But clarity creates power.
And power creates direction.

What you hold in your hands is not only a book.
It is a return to ourselves.

A return to our intelligence.
A return to our lineage.
A return to our capacity.
A return to our truth.

A return to the blueprint we were always meant to build.

You are the turning point.
You are the first chapter of a new era.
You are the beginning of a hundred-year correction.

Your family will speak differently because of you.
Your children will dream differently because of you.
Your lineage will move differently because of you.

This book ends here, but your legacy begins now.

You were never behind.
You were preparing for this moment.
Now you build forward.

ACKNOWLEDGMENTS

This book was born from a lifetime of questions, a lifetime of searching, and a lifetime of watching our people carry burdens they did not deserve.

To every Black family who ever felt behind without knowing why, this book is for you.

To the first-generation builders who carry the weight of being the example, the protector, the student, and the teacher all at once, this book is for you.

To the mothers, fathers, grandparents, and elders who held families together through forces designed to break them, this book is because of you.

To the children who will inherit a different world because of the seeds planted in this generation, this book is a promise to you.

To every ancestor whose brilliance, courage, resilience, and sacrifice are the foundation of our existence, this book is an offering.
You built, you endured, you dreamed without seeing the finish line.
We honor you by continuing what you started.

And to every reader who saw themselves somewhere in these pages, thank you.
You are proof that our story is not finished.
You are proof that the next century belongs to us.

The work continues.
The legacy continues.
The building continues.

Together, we move.

ABOUT THE AUTHOR

Brian B. Turner is a storyteller, entrepreneur, and cultural architect whose work explores the intersection of identity, economics, and generational healing. Raised in a first-generation household and navigating the pressure of being "the one who makes it," Brian spent years searching for clarity about wealth, progress, and why so many capable people feel behind.

His writing brings together history, psychology, economics, and lived experience to reveal the forces shaping Black families today and the opportunities available to those building from scratch. Through his *Built From Scratch* series, the *Always Up* podcast, BBT APPAREL, and his expanding digital platforms, Brian creates frameworks that offer structure, truth, and direction to readers who were never given a blueprint.

He writes to restore confidence, correct narratives, and help the next generation inherit knowledge instead of confusion. Brian lives in Miami, Florida, where he continues to build work that speaks to those rebuilding their lives, their families, and their future.